Eduardo Paolozzi
Recurring Themes

This exhibition has been generously sponsored by

Lufthansa

P E A R S O N

Sir Terence Conran

The Scottish Sculpture Trust is particularly grateful for assistance and support from:-

The President and Council of the Royal Scottish Academy, the Architectural Association, Julian Andrews, Stafford Cliff, George Donald, Murray Gngor, Mr & Mrs Charles Jencks, Jan Leman, Dani Karavan, The Royal College of Art, Professor Rudolf Seitz, Dr Armin Zweite, Frank Thurston.

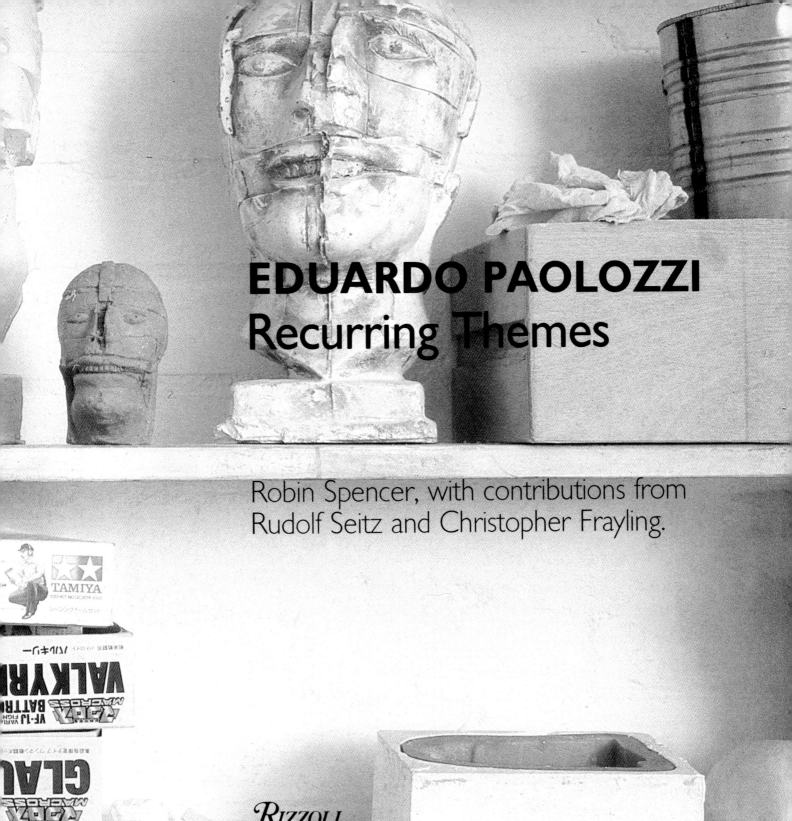

EDUARDO PAOLOZZI
Recurring Themes

Robin Spencer, with contributions from
Rudolf Seitz and Christopher Frayling.

RIZZOLI
NEW YORK

All rights reserved
Copyright © The Scottish Sculpture Trust, 1984
Published in the United States of America by Rizzoli Publications, Inc.,
712 Fifth Avenue, New York.
First published 1984
Designed by Conway Lloyd Morgan
Set in Gill Sans Light by Words & Pictures, London
Colour origination by Colorlito
Printed by Jolly & Barber Ltd, Rugby
Bound by Hunter & Foulis Ltd, Edinburgh

CONTENTS

Within each heading, the introduction has been written by Robin Spence
and section I contains sculpture; section 2, drawings and collages; section
prints and section 4, models and photographs.

Unless otherwise stated works are lent by the artist.
Sculptures are unique unless a numbered edition is noted
Dimensions in centimetres, height precedes width
For prints image size precedes paper size
Abbreviations:
s   – signed
sd   – signed and dated
inscr inscribed

PREFACE

On 7 March this year Paolozzi was sixty. In London, the Architectural Association held a dinner to mark the occasion. In Munich, Paolozzi's students at the Academy, where he is Professor of Sculpture, gave him a Japanense feast at which he presided, sitting cross-legged, and attired in the robe of a samurai warrior. It is now Edinburgh's turn to honour Paolozzi and his art, and to welcome him back to the city of his birth where he took the first steps on the road to becoming an artist. The present exhibition, at the centre of Edinburgh's 1984 International Festival, reflects not only Paolozzi's place in the wider European context but also the affection in which he is still held at home.

Preparing for the exhibition and this book has not so much incurred acknowledgements, but rather the renewal of old friendships and the making of new ones. First, nothing could have been achieved without the artist, whose art, like his friendship, is both an inspiration and a constant source of pleasure. The fact that he has entered so rich and productive a period in his work is in some small part due to the President and Council of the Royal Scottish Academy who as early as 1982 readily agreed to the exhibition being held in their galleries. Paolozzi has long regarded them as being among the finest in Europe. It is also of satisfaction to know that a reduced version of the exhibition will also be seen in other European centres, including the Lenbachhaus, Munich, whose Director, Dr Armin Zweite, has taken an active interest in planning the exhibition.

Without the generosity of sponsors and collectors, public and private, the exhibition could not have taken place. We particularly thank the Arts Council of Great Britain, the British Council, Aberdeen Art Gallery and Museum, City of Edinburgh Museums and Galleries, Glasgow Art Gallery and Museum, Leeds City Art Galleries, the Royal Academy, the Tate Gallery, the Whitworth Art Gallery, University of Manchester, as well as Zeev Aram and other anonymous lenders and the artist himself from whose collection all other works come. We have been assisted by Isi Metzstein and Marlee Robinson, the artist's personal assistant. Marlee has liaised on all aspects of the exhibition and carried out the formidable task of locating all the illustrations for this book. Robert Breen, who organised a Paolozzi exhibition in Edinburgh in 1976, brought the exhibition plans to fruition as Director of the Scottish Sculpture Trust. While Marlee Robinson and David Scruton have assisted us with aspects of the catalogue, the text has been brought vividly to life by the contributions of Christopher Frayling and Rudi Seitz who have written, with observant humour and warmth, of what it is like to be Eduardo, in and out of the lecture room and studio, in London and in Munich.

Robin Spencer and Barbara Grigor
Exhibition organisers for the Scottish Sculpture Trust

INTRODUCTION

Robin Spencer

'Art is a long word which can be stretched' Eduardo Paolozzi.

Throughout a long career Paolozzi's art has undergone notable changes. Long remembered for his Pop imagery, his art of the last fourteen years could not look more different. But the fact that artist colleagues in London called him a Surrealist thirty years ago, rather than a Pop artist, should serve as a warning to those who want to catalogue and label artists and movements too soon. In all his work, in different media, from the miniature sculpture to the large public commission, Paolozzi has maintained a unity of purpose and vision, which is rare among contemporary artists. Instead of endlessly repeating a style or an image, Paolozzi has gone on further to develop his refreshing view of the world and its contrasting cultures. He refuses to limit himself to single ideas or to artistic fashions sanctioned by the art world, on which some of his colleagues have built their careers. Thus his art has always been challenging, exciting – and prophetic. In the last fourteen years he has developed a new language for his sculpture which seems more private and personal than before. Although superficially different from previous work, the themes and subjects he treats now in sculpture can still be related to the past. In order to clarify these relationships the exhibition has been divided thematically into four sections: 'Heads and Portraits', 'From **Cleish** to **Clock**', 'Landscape in Relief', 'Heroes and Deities' and 'Studio to City Square'. For it is in these genres that Paolozzi is still vigorously and creatively working, as he has done now for forty years.

For a sculptor, Paolozzi is in fact nearly as well known for the prints he has made. Graphic art has always played an important part in the development of his sculpture, not least in the last fourteen years. Much of his recent sculpture in relief underlines an important relationship between the two media. When he first began making sculpture in the 1940s, it was the principle of impressing 'found objects' into clay which, after casting in wax and plaster, provided him with a vocabulary of design sheets for the free-standing bronze sculptures made by the lost-wax process in the 1950s. In 1961-2 his sculpture underwent a further change. Made from pre-designed elements in aluminium, the smooth engineered surfaces of his towers, still-lives and figures engaged him in a metaphorical dialogue between man and the machine, a subject which has always obsessed him. The nature of this dialogue and his attitude to the machine has been modified over the years.

This art, both formally and symbolically, is an expressive acknowledgemen[t] those changes. By concentrating on work made since 1971 the pres[ent] exhibition is an exploration of what those circumstances and concerns m[ean] for his art.

The 1960s had concluded with a rich flowering of screenprints. **Gene[ral] Dynamic Fun** of 1970, a portfolio of fifty images, celebrated a humoro[us] and often bizarre parody of urban existence. Other screen-prints, wh[ich] Paolozzi referred to as 'mental landscapes', were crammed, almost to [the] point of horror vacui, with highly coloured details of watches, charts, sp[ace] rockets, film stars and politicians.

In 1971-2 although he remained comparatively inactive as a sculptor, [the] outward appearance of Paolozzi's graphic art began to change. In contrast [to] the brilliant coloration of previous work, the photo-gravure etchings **Clo[ud] Atomic Laboratory**, made in 1971, document in stark black and white [the] way man had become mechanised both at work and at play. They sh[ow] images of robotic man, fashioned by scientific man, to simulate organic rea[lity] in circumstances of self-induced physical stress and conflict. They are liter[ally] 'mannikins for destruction', a theme touched on ten years later in the [film] Bladerunner and in a cinematic tradition which stretches back to Metrop[olis] (both films, incidentally, being favourites of Paolozzi's). In 1971 he mad[e] further allusion to the source of this idea, in his sculpture **Crash He[ad]** complete with neck bolt and chain. At the same time, in the screen-p[rint] **Mr Peanut**, the diminutive figures float across and are dwarfed b[y a] geometricised grid-like structure which Paolozzi derived from an image [of] organ music visualised in abstraction by a German artist in 1927. T[his] synaesthetic process of expressing sound through colours and shapes was [to] have profound significance for the sculpture and graphics which wo[uld] follow.

Almost simultaneously, while the implications of these ideas were be[ing] absorbed, Paolozzi was occupied with the retrospective exhibition of [his] work held at the Tate Gallery in the summer of 1971. The exhibition gave [him] an over-view of twenty-five years' works which culminated in the m[ost] inventive configurations in sculpture and graphics produced by any artist [in] that decade. For this occasion the large three-part sculpture **Hamlet i[n a] Japanese Manner** was specially painted. (It is seen in the present exhibiti[on] stripped to the base material). For the exhibition in 1971 he made a numb[er] of important visual statements which at the time were not taken seriously [by] critics.

Only now can their significance be properly gauged. Never afraid of taki[ng] on the art establishment on his own terms, Paolozzi let it be known that [he] had little or no interest in what the art world was then enthusing over. H[e] constructed (beautifully) a **Minimal Snail on a Primary Structure**; and [a] spoof pastel-striped Noland-style field painting, complete with parrot on [a] stand and a set of plaster gnomes stencilled 'concrete abstractionism' a[nd] other satirical soubriquets, taken from critical terminology then current. I[n a] giant skip constructed of aluminium and marked 'Cloud Atomic Laborato[ry]' were castings of discarded sculpture, to which Paolozzi later added t[he] image of an archetypal victim – a giant bust of President John Kenned[y]. Images of destruction in the form of painted bombs and a pile of gold ing[ots] completed the ensemble which seemed (in retrospect) to have mo[re] relevance for the socio-political 1980s than the conceptually-minimal 197[0s]

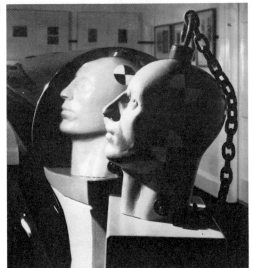

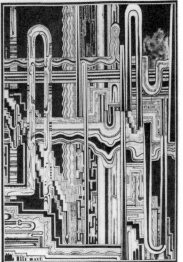

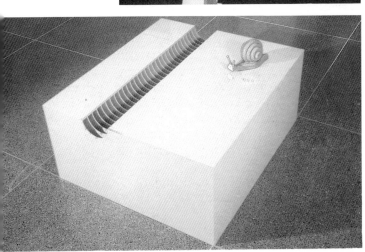

The potential for world-wide destruction and the increasing waste of human resources are mutually reciprocal features of life in the late twentieth century. Paolozzi sees the acknowledgement of this state of affairs, its causes and effects, as being inextricably linked to the machine's ubiquitous role and the effect it has on all our lives. It is a theme which is central to his art. For Paolozzi, an act of destruction, either by himself or someone else, must usually precede an act of creation. It may result in an improvement on a previous statement, or be used as a means of transforming it into something 'wonderful and extraordinary that is neither nonsensical nor morally edifying'.[2]

Paolozzi has described himself growing up in Edinburgh in the 1920s and 1930s, as part of a culture 'which threw nothing away'.[3] He is amazed by the thousands of magazine images which lie unexamined and unused outside the Munich Academy of Fine Arts. He takes pride in the fact that most of his recent wood reliefs are modelled from off-cuts unwanted by other artists

Hommage à Bruckner, 1977

Hunterian Gallery doors

Cleish Castle interior

and to be found in a skip behind the Royal College of Art in London. They are of use, it would seem, to no one but himself; but out of them he can build complex visual metaphors, at no cost other than to his own inventive genius.

The principal materials for his sculpture once belonged in another context to something or someone else; a radio, a piano or a plaster cast after the Laocoön. In two dimensions, his collages might include a magazine image about wireless communication, the biography of a composer or a catalogue to the Greek sculpture in the British Museum. Before selecting these images he allows himself little time to distinguish between what is considered art, and what is not. What matters is bringing together, in a unique way, unfamiliar items into a new context. Only then can a truly artistic statement be made. Paolozzi philosphically accepts the historical inevitability of a divided culture he has fallen heir to. In the preface to **Cloud Atomic Laboratory** he wrote: 'a difficulty in assessing aesthetic value in these works is emphasised by the monolithic concepts concerning all the GREAT MECHANICAL ARTS . . . The schism that separates Space-Age engineering, technical photography, film-making and types of street art from fine art activities is for many people/ artists unbridgeable.'

If he has long resigned himself to the social and political forces which have helped to shape the status quo of today's art world, Paolozzi's answer in his own art is far from being a passive one. He offers us a unique view of how we are located – and at times locked – into our own cultures; and how we use the artefacts of work and leisure – which we sometimes call art – to surround, distract and improve ourselves.

Meanwhile, in 1972, the formal and expressive possibilities offered by the new geometry led him once again to work in relief, first for the ceiling of Cleish Castle, Scotland; and then in 1975 in Berlin, to create independent works in bronze, plaster, resin and wood. Other public commissions in Germany and Britain followed, including the doors for the Hunterian Art Gallery, Glasgow University, which opened in 1980. In order to launch his new language for relief sculpture, which initially was based on a graphic source, Paolozzi made hundreds of pencil drawings during the years 1971-3.

These drawings provided him with a suitable vocabulary for the new picto formulae he was evolving for sculpture. Although two-dimensional, mos the drawings convey, through changing angles and degrees of light a shade, the implication of shallow three-dimensional depth. In his first relie for the ceiling of Cleish Castle, vestigial cog wheels and mechanical shap counterpoint the geometry. They are a distant reminder of the 'ready-ma elements which were encrusted in the detritus-laden surfaces of his figu sculpture in the 1950s. As the handling of the new language became mo confident and assured, these forms became absorbed by the geometry u they disappeared from the reliefs altogether. It appeared that after two an half decades of making sculpture with anthropomorphic references Paolo was creating an abstract sculpture devoid of metamorphic associations. fact this was not so. For no sooner was he in top gear, with wood and plas reliefs multiplying as fast as they could be cast into bronze, than he bega series of great screenprints which were to take him two years to comple from 1974 to 1976.

This was **Calcium Light Night**, dedicated to the American compos Charles Ives. These screenprints are to Paolozzi's relief sculpture what t pioneering **As is When** series of screenprints was to the aluminiu sculpture of the previous decade. Across the decades the two ser symmetrically share the language of the sculpture to which they respectiv relate. Whereas **As is When** took as its subject aspects of the life of Ludw Wittgenstein, and posed philosphical questions about the nature of art a language, **Calcium Light Night** suggests a synaesthetic way of expressi sensations in art other than by sight. Paolozzi particularly admires Char Ives for the way he expanded the European symphonic tradition by darin grafting on to it marching songs, brass band music and popular tunes fro American folk music. That all this was achieved by an American insuran agent with otherwise conventional tastes appeals to Paolozzi, as did t idiosyncratic liking of Wittgenstein, while living in England, for Betty Grab and Mickey Mouse. Like Paolozzi himself, an Italian brought up in Scotlan both composer and philosopher found themselves alienated by the cultu conventions of the respective countries in which they found themselv

8

concurrent with **Calcium Light Night** came other related works, such as the **Ravel Suite** of etchings, which pays homage to a composer long admired by Paolozzi; and later in the decade, the sculpture **Homage à Bruckner**, with similar iconography, for the town of Linz in Austria.

There are technical differences between making the pre-conceived, pre-selected engineered elements of the 1960s, and the more intuitively crafted wood components of the 1970s, although both methods of working share similar conceptual aims. The aluminium sculptures required a draughtsman's blueprint before they could be realised, and required sophisticated welding techniques in production. The reliefs need to be worked by hand, cut and sawed, sanded and finally composed, using judgments made by the eye and brain simultaneously. Not surprisingly, in the last ten years, Paolozzi has also turned to wood engraving and etchings, where decisions made by the eye can be more finely controlled than when printing big editions of complex screenprints.

His most recent sculpture and graphic art is in many respects closer in spirit to the work he was doing twenty-five years ago than to the less intimate sculpture of the 1960s: for example, he has returned to the subject of the portrait head and the figure, which preoccupied him in the 1950s. In a recent radio interview, he describes these reappearing interests as 'old work pressing through'.[4] In 1971 he readily admitted that his robot-like bronzes from the past might understandably be likened to the way figures could look after the bomb went off.[5] Yet in the 1950s the idea of conflict and annihilation on a global scale could not be seriously engaged by an artist and his public as it can be today; or even as Paolozzi saw it in 1971 when he choreographed his sardonic tableau noir at the Tate Gallery. Never before have the polarities of creation and destruction been so far apart. And never before in Paolozzi's art have they been made so apparent.

There are serious and sonorous warnings to be found in Paolozzi's most recent portrait heads; and in one or two of his recent etchings he has permitted himself a rare political aside. How can today's artists contemplate such horror, confront and depict it in their art, as a permanent warning against a tomorrow that one day may never come? It is a question that only a great artist can ask himself; and in art provide an answer. Perhaps by sheer creativity, rather than any real political involvement, Picasso, in this century, addressed himself convincingly to the question. There seems little doubt that for several years Paolozzi too has been asking it, at times implicitly, at others more explicitly. In 1979 he wrote a text 'Junk and the New Arts and Crafts Movement' which depressingly sets forth a gloomy view for mankind's future and the imaginary modernistic culture that might soon accompany it.[6] In his art, gone forever is a celebration of technology or a playful parody of the machine.

Paolozzi's reliefs have finally consigned the once-thought friendly face of the computer-console to the dust heap; his graphics banish the print-out circuit to the floor. The reliefs, softly coloured in shades of violet and green, sing a more celestial song and seem to rest on a plane far above the simple, basic materials out of which they are made. They are brittle artefacts, delicately crafted, from a civilization in the process of involuntarily transporting itself towards a destination yet unknown. But in reality, their destiny will doubtless be the museum. Inside its shattered walls a future archaeologist may one day discover several small mummified heads, made in

Modern Mechanix, 1935   German ethnology book

the late twentieth century, and almost indistinguishable from those found at Pompeii. Dusted, they may be re-displayed alongside other portrait heads, also preserved intact, but which give evidence of having once undergone severe facial surgery. The origins of these heads cannot be established with any degree of certainty. Although made in the image of man their features are confused and bear the scars of various ethnic types from different parts of the world. Their original purpose is unsure.

Since Lessing in the eighteenth century debated the volume of the scream from the Laocoön, and Eisenstein and Francis bacon depicted it in our own time, no artist, with the exception of Paolozzi, has expressed the manifest pain of our condition with such force; at the same time qualifying it with marks which are traditionally at the artist's disposal: thus pastel watercolour delicately streaks the white plaster head reproduced on the cover of this book. Punk-classical, east-west hybrids; some traced with the wire technology assaulting our sense organs, these heads have 'the heart-rending expression of the age', which a century ago Vincent Van Gogh saw in his portrait of Dr. Gachet. Made from the lingering remnants of the classical tradition and the modern symbolism of the King's Road, they create a new breed in the image of man. Each head, by a small degree, is unlike its fellow. In these differences lie their individuality, an unending permutation of detail for future development.

A German ethnological study of heads, variations on a racial theme (which would have appealed to Francis Bacon), is in Paolozzi's collection. Recently, he has also unearthed a long-lost competition to reassemble scrambled photo-fit heads, run by Modern Mechanix and Inventions Magazine in 1935-6. He now thinks it may have been one starting point, among others, for the **Time** collage portraits he made in 1952 and 1953, which are the graphic ancestors to his recent sculpture. Rather, they are layers of cultural experience, comingling with the history of art, which he filters and synthesises to make new truths. 'There is nothing new in art, that has not been attempted before at one time or another, in antiquity, or by Picasso. For a young artist to claim for his work total originality is as self-deluding as it is arrogant.'[7]

9

Often Paolozzi talks of his admiration for Rodin, and his habit of obliviously strewing drawings at his feet as he walked; drawings of symbolic figures, portraits, monuments, classical and Chinese, moving and still; not caring for their individual importance or immediate finality, only for the flux of ideas towards which he advanced a new sculptural image out of plaster or clay.

Paolozzi is now bringing to completion some figure studies he has been working on for several years: the first hint of one – **Torso** – is in this exhibition. Their origins will seem as obscure as that of the heads, with which their emaciated forms, with enlarged ribcases, will eventually join forces, in a series of variations reminiscent of Rodin's practice of utilising a repertoire of interchangeable limbs. Unlike conventional images of or by Western man, these figures promise to be among the most telling expressions of our over-developed culture – but, by the paradox that always accompanies great art, a clue for its advancement as well.

Robin Spencer June 1984

Notes

1. The assemblage **Thunder and Lightning, Flies with Jack Kennedy** was shown at the Royal Academy, London, 1972, and is now in the Palazzo Reale, Milan.
2. Edouard Roditi, **Dialogues on Art**, London 1960 (rev. ed. Santa Barbara, 1980), p. 160.
3. Eduardo Paolozzi, BBC, Radio 3, March 1984.
4. **Ibid.**
5. Frank Whitford, 'Paolozzi', **Art and Design BBC Radiovision**, 1971, p. 12.
6. Catalogue of the exhibition 'Eduardo Paolozzi, Collages, Prints, Sculptures', Talbot Rice Art Centre, Edinburgh University, 1979.
7. In conversation, May 1984.

Eduardo Paolozzi at the RCA (Maximum Energy Pile)

Christopher Frayling

Eduardo Paolozzi has been a tutor in the Department of Ceramics at the Royal College of Art since 1968. Before that, he taught in the Textile Design Department at the Central School of Art and Design, and he combines his Tutorship in Ceramics with a Professorship in Sculpture at Munich Academy – 14 days consecutively in London, 14 days consecutively in Munich. It's an appropriate combination for an artist and maximum energy pile who has spent his adult life challenging the barriers between the arts, or inventing new categories of his own. And apart from anything else, it's made him something of an authority on the giveway magzines which are supplied by British Airways and Lufthansa: 'in High Life, on British Airways, the photography banal and reeks of parochialism. The literary style represents shabby journalism . . . the Lufthansa Bordbuch is another idea – bilingual and with no 'personalities' but a team of highly intelligent professionals employing specially commissioned photographers. Everything fits together like a super clock. Even the maps are better designed.'

The observations on High Life have often been made: someone once said that it's the only aircraft giveway where passengers read the sickbag and vomit over the magazine. And the preference for Ulm – rather than a Fleet Street version of Merrie England – will be shared by many practising artists and designers. But the image is **pure Eduardo**: one can imagine him sitting in the plane somewhere between Heathrow and Munich, feverishly cutting up the magazines with some cardboard and cow gum perched on his plastic tray, listening through ear-phones to jazz selections from the multi-track in-flight entertainment channel, blowing up a head of steam on the vexed question of English 'parochialism', and all the time from take-off to touch down free-associating as only he can in readiness for his tutorials in London, Munich.

Touching down at the RCA: in addition to his work in the Ceramic Department – selecting new students, firing young ceramicists with his enthusiasms and helping them to discover their own, assessing their work evolving new projects (in a variety of media) in the studios, enabling the students to build bridges between the world of the College and the world of everywhere else – Eduardo often gives lectures and presents 'multi vocative' events to other schools and departments (among them Photography, Graphics, Cultural History, and on one famous occasion to both members of the RCA branch of the Friends of the Earth). His teaching seems to be based on two fundamental principles: that it is important to learn from **within a discipline**, and that it is equally important to be aware of the many cultural influences and cross-currents which may in the end be **a challenge to that discipline**. One of his colleagues in Ceramics has said that these two principles may be expressed as 'hitting the nail right on the head' and 'teaching at a tangent'. Some of the catch-phrases which Eduardo uses in both aspects of his teaching have become part of the folklore of the RCA: 'the BA syndrome', 'evening class uncollected', 'it's pure Cheam', 'the Cinderella Complex of the crafts', 'I saw this in a bookshop in Munich and I immediately thought of you', 'why can't the College be open on Christmas Day?', 'don't throw that out', 'it's a paradox', and, most of all, '**give it a whirl**'. He is extremely loyal and generous to all his students – especially those who are as committed to their work as he is, and as tough-minded when it comes to confronting the mega-visual contours of the everyday media landscape: he is just as likely (more likely, actually) to take them to the stores of the Museum of Mankind ('did you know they have Malinowski's false teeth in the basement?'), or the conservation workshops of the Aircraft Museum ('these are **real** crafstmen') – places they wouldn't otherwise think of visiting – as he is to do a conducted tour of the latest exhibition which is all the rage with the Burlington set. During his stay in California in 1968, Eduardo visited very few art galleries or museums: instead he is reputed to have gone to Disneyland, to the wax museums of San Francisco and Los Angeles, to Frederick's Lingerie Showrooms and Paramount Studios, to the University of California Computer Centre, Stanford University's linear accelerator, the Douglas Aircraft Company in Santa Monica and the General Motors Assemblyline in Hayward. Today his RCA students will tend to be exposed to an equivalent range of interests: material for the **bricoleur**, and essential experience for an artist or designer living in 1984 and beyond. I can well recall going to see Ridley Scott's Bladerunner (1982) with Eduardo and a member of the up and coming **jeunesse dorée de design**: after the film was over, Eduardo asked this gentleman of taste what he thought about it. 'I'm just going home to listen to some Scarlatti to clear my palate', was the reply. The expression on Eduardo's face was **priceless**. He'd particularly enjoyed Bladerunner because the replicant manufacturer's workshop was so very like his own studio in London.

PAOLOZZI IN THE LECTURE THEATRE
(HISTORY AS BUNK, AFTER HENRY)

Imagine, if you will, Dr Henry Frankenstein giving a magic-lantern show to his young colleagues in the Gothick setting of Goldstadt's medical college, after doing a spot of needle work on Elsa Lanchester's/Mary Shelley's cadaver (it doesn't take **that** much imagination, for it was another Edinburgh man of Italian descent who wrote the first vampyre story on the same 'wet, dismal' evening in Geneva, and anyway the scene, or a version of it, has appeared in the first reel of countless Universal pictures). The Faculty expects to be reassured by the folk-wisdom of the eighteenth-century scientific academies, which won't upset the local priest and certainly won't upset the burgomaster played by Lionel Belmore. Fritz (or is it Igor?) dims the illumination, lights the candle behind the glass-painted images, and the young doctors are respectfully silent. Watch this.

VAUCANSON'S GILDED COPPER DIGESTING DUCK, CONSTRUCTED TO PROVE THE THESIS THAT PEOPLE ARE REALLY SOFT MACHINES; IT EATS IT DRINKS IT SWIMS IT DIGESTS BISCUITS IT EVEN DRINKS THREE GLASSES OF WINE; EACH WING CONTAINS OVER FOUR HUNDRED MOVING PARTS: shouts of 'quack! quack! quack!': AN ENGRAVED CUT-AWAY PLAN, FROM DIDEROT'S ENCYCLOPEDIA, OF THE VARIOUS TOOLS AND JIGS USED BY THE WORKERS IN A PIN FACTORY: mutterings about the wealth of the nations: PRINT OF AN AEROSTATIC EXPERIMENT MADE AT LYONS IN 1784, WITH A BALLOON 100 FEET IN DIAMETER, DESTROYED BY PEASANTS WHO THINK THE BALLOON IS A MOON/A PARISIAN LADY WEARING HER 'CHAPEAU AU BALLON': confused wolf-whistles: PRINT OF TWO TRAVELLERS FLOATING IN THE AIR, WITH AEROSTATIC COSTUMES AND MANIVOLES IN THEIR HANDS; THEY BOTH HAVE CORK JACKETS TO HELP THEM SKIM ALONG THE WATER/ EROTIC DETAIL OF J-J ROUSSEAU SITTING ON A CHAIR WITH HIS BREECHES DOWN, AND MADAME DE WARENS OR MAMAN STANDING ACROSS HIM AT LES CHARMETTES: slow hand-clapping: ENGRAVING FROM THE PHYSICA SACRA BY JOHANN JAKOB SCHEUCHZER OF THE HUMAN HEART, SHOWING A RUSTIC SWAIN PINING FOR HIS LOVED-ONE BENEATH A TREE, TWO COILS OF FLEXIBLE TUBING, THE VESSELS, VALVES, MUSCU-LATURE AND ANATOMICAL OPENINGS OF THE HUMAN HEART IN DIFFERENT SCALES AND PERSPECTIVES, A MECHANICAL TWO-CHAMBERED PUMPING DEVICE AND A QUOTATON FROM PSALM 32/VIEW OF THE CROSSING OF THE RIVER SEINE, BENEATH THE PONT NEUF, ON DRY FEET, BY MEANS OF ELASTIC SHOES, JANUARY 1874: both the priest and the burgomaster walk out, talking in stage-whispers about the decline and fall of the house of Frankenstein: THE JACQUET-DROZ MECHANICAL CHILD SCRIBE WHO HAS BEEN WRITING 'COGITO ERGO SUM' OVER AND OVER AGAIN SINCE 1770; IF ITS MECHANISM IS CHANGED IT CAN DRAW, IN INK, DELIGHTFUL TAKE-AWAY LANDSCAPES OF THE NEUCHATEL COUNTRYSIDE; INSIDE ITS HUMANOID SHELL, A COMPLEX SYSTEM OF COG-WHEELS, CYLINDERS, STEEL CAMS, LEVERS, RODS AND GEARS HELPS IT TO PERFORM CONTINUOUSLY WITH A FEATHER QUILL-PEN; PERHAPS WE SHOULD PUT A FEW OF THEM IN THE ATELIERS OF GOLDSTADT ACADEMY OF ARTS AND SEE IF ANYONE NOTICES THE DIFFERENCE: nobody is laughing: PARACELSUS LECTURING AT THE UNIVERSITY OF BASLE ON HOW TO CREATE A HOMUNCULUS WITH THE AID OF ALCHEMY, MID-SIXTEENTH CENTURY: a general movement towards the door, knocking Fritz (or is it Igor?) against Elsa Lanchester's cadaver; only two young doctors remain – to ask the lecturer if they can join his research team; it's a crazy idea but it just might work; the cadaver's scarred right hand begins to twitch … **IT'S ALIVE!**

André Breton, writing about 'the castle question' and 'the beauty of the marvellous' in 1936, wrote that 'Human psychism in its most universal aspect has found in the Gothick castle and its accessories a point of fixation so precise that it becomes essential to discover what would be the equivalent for our own period (everything leads us to believe that there is no question of it being a factory)'. Eduardo Paolozzi, in his infamous 'multi-evocative' magic-lantern show of images to the first meeting of the Independent Group at the ICA (1952), and since then at numerous lectures and events for the students at the RCA, has been engaged on the same voyage of discovery. The images, shuffled like a pack of Charles Eames playing cards, appear side-by-side on the big screen, sometimes accompanied by soft jazz piped through the PA system. Blam, blam, blam. They come from the worlds of technology, scientific research, popular culture, design and fine art – a diapositive scrap-book to be shared with and reassembled by the audience. As one critic has written about Paolozzi lectures 'why show such fragments of such familiar material? It takes the right frame of mind to interpret such images and to perceive their rich layers of meaning. It also demands a new kind of non-linear interpretation, for Paolozzi is dealing with visual experience in a way close to the manner in which a multitude of disparate images bombard us in everyday life . . .' A recent event, entitled **Junk and the New Arts and Crafts Movement**, was advertised within the RCA by one of Eduardo's **Blueprints for a New Museum**: an American bomber, a satellite, a bicycle, an Action Man, some printed circuitry, a mechanical horse, a fish, three bikini-clad girls riding on a bomb, and the Hellenistic Laocoon group from which the philospher Lessing took the title of his essay on aesthetics (a favourite image) all float in the zero-gravity of Cologne Cathedral. The images (like the lecture itself) encouraged lateral thinking about the function of museums today – the Boilerhouse had just opened – about Ruskin and the crafts – 'is this slide of a cracked fragment of a pot from ancient Greece or from last year's Degree Show?' – and about the still conventional boundaries between 'fine' and 'coarse' art: the images were out of scale with each other, which made the audience think about their scale, and the impact of the event depended to a large extent on the audience making the connections for themselves. As Eduardo said after the lecture, 'If one or two students start thinking or looking in a new way, then the event's been a success. They are usually the students who **don't** ask questions'. Since the questions are often (too often) about the past – put by casual observers who are writing **yet another essay** on 'The Roots of Pop Art. Discuss' – the comment is understandable. Eduardo added that he'd just been to a lecture which was a knockout, by an art historian who spent two hours talking abut the details in one painting. So events like **Junk** aren't, of course, the only way of lecturing effectively about/through art – but they are the way which happens to suit him best.

POSTSCRIPT: PAOLOZZI AND THE SKIP
(No waste/RCA Atomic Laboratory)

In the 1971 Eduardo Paolozzi retrospective at the Tate Gallery, one of the most controversial exhibits was an aluminium skip filled with rejected sculptures and castings, entitled **Waste**. A critic at the time wrote that 'by filling a hopper (read: skip) with earlier, discarded sculpture, Paolozzi demonstrates that even his own work is not above criticism.' If Eduardo's

teaching in the studios at the RCA is anything to go by, that critic was ver very wide of the mark. For there is another skip, not aluminium but neve mind, located round the back of the College (just beneath the red spray-gu message of the punk period ART IS DEAD – GOOD) which has come t play an essential role in the day-to-day work of the Department of Ceramic It achieved a certain notoriety a few years back when some emissaries from the Department of Education and Science walked straight past the skip at th wrong moment (in other words before Eduardo has taken the students to first) and penned an over-hasty report to the Minister, entitled **Waste**. Th College skip contains all the 'junk' which is discarded by most of the Desig Departments during the course of a working week At the moment, th Ceramics studios are lined with sheets of 2 x 2 boarding which went into th skip after the Albert exhibition of last Autumn. But at other times of the year visitors might have glimpsed PLASTIC BREAD-TRAYS (ASSORTED) LIDS FROM TEA-CHESTS, BITS AND PIECES FROM A DISCARDEL TELEVISION SET (NOTABLY THE GUN FROM THE BACK OF A TUBE), A LENGTH OF PLASTIC HOSE, PLASTICATED WIRE IN SPIRALS, A PENCIL BOX AND A VEGETABLE RACK (PROVENANC UNKNOWN). They tend to remain in the Department – as teaching-aids Paolozzi-style – for students to look at, think about, draw, use in their work dismantle, build upon, or transform into another material. On one folklori occasion, Eduardo came across a derelict piano (**not** in the skip), the wires keys, hammers, casing and frame of which underwent the Frankenstein treatment with the students, for several weeks; a treasure-trove of found objects-in-the-process-of-becoming-significant-images. Ruskin's favourite teaching-aid, when he lectured at Oxford, was a box full of newspaper cuttings, cut-out engravings, and items from the scrap-book. Mr Chip preferred a black-board. Eduardo Paolozzi uses the skip. For the skip ma contain clay tablets, as they say, unearthed in a sunken empire town . . .

A KRAZY KATALYST

In the Summerson Report of 1964, which helped to found the curren system of art and design education in England, it is asserted (quite rightly that 'a brilliant practising artist or designer is not necessarily a natural teacher In this, as in so much else, Eduardo Paolozzi is the great exception to the rule As Krazy Katalyst, as highly gifted teacher, a loyal ally, Paolozzi is one of those **rarissime** artists whose teaching is congruent with his work, just as his wor is congruent with his teaching.

Keep giving it a whirl, Eduardo.

Christopher Frayling
Professor and Head of the Department of Cultural History
Royal College of Art

(Thanks to David Queensberry, David Hamilton, John Miller and Frank Whitford. The quotation about airline magazines is from Campaign November 1982: 'The Images that Inspire Today's Artists' by Paolozzi. Al the images in the **Frankenstein** lecture could, in fact, have been shown by him in summer 1816, and they all exist somewhere).

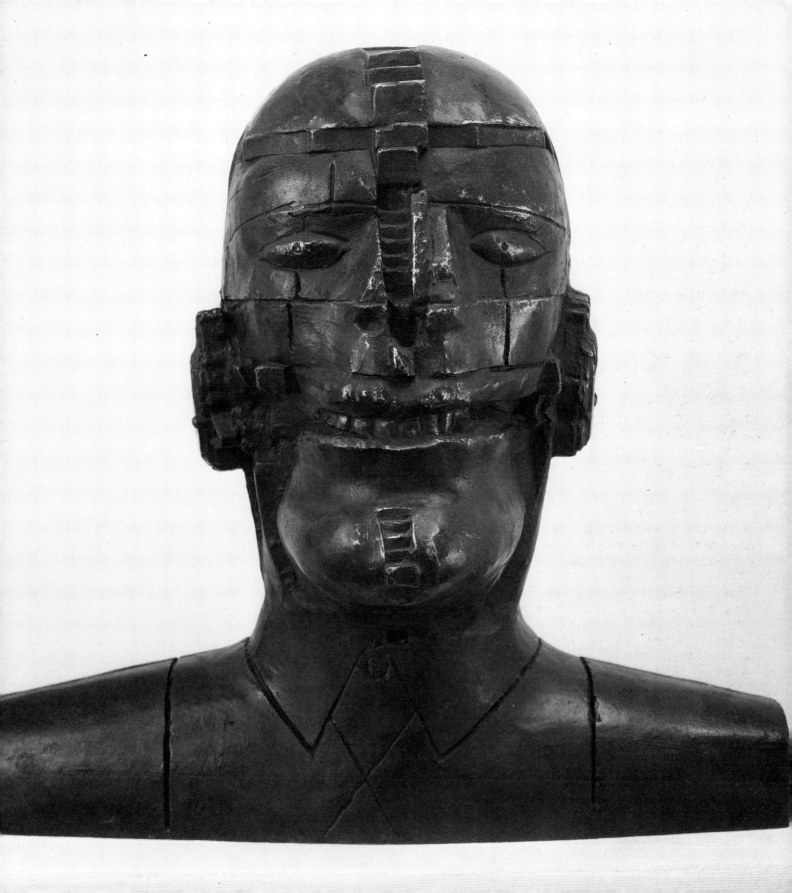

AI.13

III BI.23
DI.6

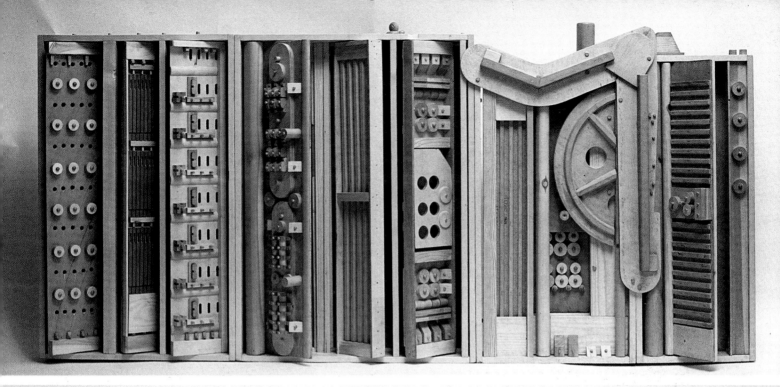

duardo Paolozzi at the Munich Academy of Fine Arts,
Ir Rudolf Seitz, President of the Academy.

In November 1st 1981 Eduardo Paolozzi succeeded Robert Jakobsen as rofessor of Sculpture at the Munich Academy of Fine Arts. A special ontract was devised to enable Eduardo Paolozzi to continue his teaching at e Royal College of Art in London; he spends about two weeks in Munich ree or four times each semester – a period of intense activity for him and s students.

duardo loves to give presents. You can hardly meet him without being anded at least a poster or a book or a catalogue. He usually has folders aiting for students or colleagues with cuttings for collage or photo-copies of ewspaper articles and pictures. All his friends belong to an invisible ycelium, ever-present in Eduardo's world. This is especially true of his udents, about whom he knows a great deal, so that while he does his own vork, little stacks accumulate about him: bits and pieces for Svava or Stefan r Urs and the rest.

The Academy also received a present, a sort of dowry: Eduardo donated large collection of his graphic work to which he is constantly adding. The cademy is very proud of this collection and has exhibited it at the British ouncil in Munich and at the Berlin Academy of Science and Technology.

here are some very interesting young artists in Eduardo's class. All distinctly dividual, some have come to sculpture by way of other art forms, such as heatre, performance and film. An international hotch-potch, there are udents from Iceland, Japan and Switzerland, Italy, Greece, Turkey, the rgentine and Czechoslovakia, as well as from Germany and, not least, ritain. They are a big family, with internal disagreements, but always ready to resent a united front when necessary. Then they will gather their forces and isplay a range of imagination and creative energy that confirms the group's ombined talent.

Once they mounted an exhibition in a matter of hours on the theme of ne 'Lever Arch File', which they explored from every imaginable angle, in very conceivable variation. Bursting with ideas, it was highly praised.

IV

But it isn't always easy. Eduardo is a very hard worker and uses his own work as the departure point for his teaching. Initially the students found this puzzling: no formal classes or crits, and individual attention for everyone – since their work is 'individual'. Group discussions go on whether Eduardo is there or not. They don't need to have him around for that. How then does it really work? All his students tell of similar experiences. When they show their work, Eduardo looks at it and makes a few remarks – usually encouraging – reaches for a book or an object and that's it: they're off on a stimulating, multi-level, thought-provoking dialogue. By the end, the student is is an an state of helpless confusion, his head buzzing with ideas which will take time to settle and shake down into an intelligible form. Eduardo has opened a new door onto an unexplored plane, where ideas can begin and go on developing. There is no system. Finished works are mere staging-posts in a continuous process, there are no 'ends'. It is the means that count.

It isn't always easy for young artists to cope with these demands on their independence and self-reliance, as they need to learn to think hard and be very receptive.

V

Eduardo teaches by means of metaphors and anaologies. I remember once finding Eduardo deep in conversation with Harry, one of his students. They talked about Bomarzo, drawings, theatre, with the radio in the background playing music from the Tokyo Kabuki Theatre. The subject was the Laocoon. Eduardo had made some photocopies, but they paid them scant attention. Allusion was piled on allusion as they worked their way around the subject indirectly, so that it seemed more like a class in Zen. Eduardo often takes paradoxes to stimulate, provoke or at least unsettle his students and so reveal an entirely new dimension of possibilities.

There are some drawings on the classroom wall, put up by Eduardo: Mishima is there, a drawing sketching out the proportions, evidence of one of those multi-dimensional dialogues that tap new resources, leaving the student in a trance.

During these conversations Eduardo usually refers to some of his own drawings and collages. They are his best means of communication, depending less on words than on images. Some of this work will be re-cycled and his ready-mades are likely to appear in his students' collages and assemblages.

VI

Like all his studios, the Munich one is full of all kinds of objects, though it is rather more organised than the Chelsea one. He sets himself specific projects for Munich, which multiply day by day. In Munich he tends to work late at night or else start early in the morning. Most of his designs for the Tottenham Court Road Tube Station in London were developed in the Munich studio. Recently he has been working on variations, enlargements and reductions of plaster models. Every surface is completely covered, the only clear space left is the bed in the far corner, and even that is surrounded by a hedge of art materials, rolls of paper and other objects. The typewriter takes up another corner, – the 'office'. When his assistant Marlee Robinson is in Munich, the demands of bureaucracy are dealt with: all the paperwork that distract from real work. She despatches it all with charm, energy and incomparable efficiency.

VII

Eduardo knows all the Munich museums intimately. On Sundays he goes to his favourite, the Glyptothek, early, before the crowds. Some of his students might go along too. He analyses and re-analyses the Barberini Faun, going through reams of paper. He gets annoyed if too many onlookers gather round, peering over his shoulder, but a quick sketch of a giant penis soon despatches even the most persistent of them.

He has been spending a lot of time taking students to the Stadtmuseum. The attraction is the collection of musical instruments from all over the world. They draw, analyse and try them out. Then they design instruments of their own to provide music for an animated film they are making in co-operation with the School of Film and Television.

VIII

The museum is the place to spark off special interests, new ideas. This is as true for Eduardo as it is for his students. He wanders along gathering ideas to be transformed in the Paolozzi process. Now and then on Saturday mornings he will take students to the lecture theatre in the Academy to look at slides of his and the students' work, along with all kinds of other subjects: junk yards, moon probes, automobile parts, power stations, and much more. Little is said. The image is their language, sequences of colliding images create their own commentary, their own terms of reference. Like in the museum, the key work is 'look'.

Eduardo is aiming for an awareness of visual language common to all, for his students to use in their work. What they must do is look, grasp and use, use, use what they see.

IX

His assistant, Andreas, says that to understand Eduardo, you have to work with him. In this context everything falls into place: the way he handles materials, breaks away the edges of a leaky plaster cast, picks up quite ordinary objects, places them together, using them as building blocks to let new ideas emerge from paradoxes of seemingly meaningless combinations, where there is no obvious logical connection. Perhaps this explains his fondness for Munich's Karl Valentin: 'I don't remember if it was yesterday or on the fifth floor'. This essentially imaginative language can only succeed when it is compressed. If students are to benefit from the combination of humour and seriousness that typifies Eduardo's work, they have to be accomplices. The result is not a production line of mini-Paolozzis, but highly individual artists, with a strong sense of how and where their own creativity can best function.

X

When Eduardo decided that the Academy needed a papermaking studio, he was confronted by two points of opposition: money and space. A few days later a Hollander was delivered. The dream had become reality. A gift from Eduardo. Naturally a space was found and a paper-making and paper sculpture experimental workshop was set up. Eduardo had felt the need for

something different alongside the traditional materials, something that pose new problems, demanding fresh solutions, where tradition could provide n easy answers.

Quite unexpectedly an excellent, lively exhibition emerged from th activity, attracting many visitors when it was shown in the Academy's larg hall and later at the Royal College of Art in London and the Kunstverein Uberlingen. It seemed to mark a new beginning, with a wealth of ideas read to break the surface.

XI

Eduardo loves having friends to dinner. Sometimes he will cook in the studi And whenever he appears in the local restaurants, they know there will soc be a crowd. Stories are told, there are arguments, jokes and a lot of fun – th mycelium is at work again.

He is host to the students too. I have never seen him so much as drink cup of coffee alone. But they won't sponge on him. Every now and then, th will invade his studio with a huge pot of spaghetti. Bottles of wine appear an they talk, bringing in visitors, too, long into the night. Objects are brought ou discussed, sketches are drawn and so it continues with everyone taking pa An exchange in the true sense of the word.

Eduardo has many stories to tell, so many first hand anecdotes abo famous artists – Picasso taking coloured pencils to 'finish' a Matisse drawin Brancusi . . .

XII

Eduardo detests long meetings, with arguments about self-inflicte problems. He hardly ever says anything. Once he even kept his 'Walkma headphones on. How I envied him. He cunningly told the meeting that I was learning German, but I'm sure there was something more interestir playing, judging from his expression. At the end of another meeting he ha finished a stack of drawings.

Eduardo as a colleague is loyal, honest, friendly and concerned. H students are devoted to him and very conscious of the great value of the relationship with him. Andreas says that Eduardo is even more important t him as a friend than as a professor. The others agree.

Andreas is helping Eduardo to pack. There are two cases this time, on inside the other. He stuffs something into a sock: 'That'll give the something to look for at Customs'.

Heads and Portraits

The interesting thing is . . . one comes back to original obsessions; or perhaps the original obsession always lies under the surface, so that I'm actually doing heads again which, instead of having detritus, have parts of an experience which is previous work pressing through . . .

Eduardo Paolozzi, BBC, Radio 3, March 1984.

Piscator, 1981

Just as Francis Bacon pursued the painted scream, so Paolozzi with his recent portrait heads appears to be interested in exploring the anguished **tête d'expression**. The history of this tradition certainly interests him, since it is a genre which lies outside the mainstream of portrait sculpture; and recently he has represented the grotesque heads of the German sculptor Franz Xavier Messerschmidt in a satirical print **A New Spirit in Painting**.

Paolozzi often makes sculpture by bringing an object or symbol from a tradition which is familiar into physical conjuction with one which is not. In so doing he produces art which speaks a new language.

Under the skin of his recent portraits lie the maps and clues to other cultures. One indicates by its title a dedication to the Japanese writer Yukio Mishima, who by ritually taking his own life symbolically reaffirmed ancient Japanese lore and resistance to Western influence, a metaphor for the survival of a culture transcending personal annihilation. The portrait is scarred by occidental features interleaved with oriental ones of a Samurai caste. A cultural hybrid, it suggests that while Western and Eastern ideologies for ordinary men may be mutually exclusive, there are no such boundaries for the artist who can see beyond them.

The dissection of eyes, mouths, noses, brows and chins from various plaster heads, classical as well as modern, their reassembly and recasting to make new portraits, also represents for Paolozzi an essential paradox in art: that destruction must come before creation.

'The word collage is inadequate as a description because the concept should include 'damage, erase, destroy, deface and transform all parts of a metaphor for the creative act itself'.[1]

Like the two-and-a-half-foot high head of Jack Kennedy which Paolozzi made twelve years ago and placed in an aluminium skip together with his discarded sculpture, the **Portrait of a Japanese Writer** is a 'hero-myth cast off'.[2] It carries the Nietzschian overtones sensed in Boccioni's Futurist sculpture, and in the art which the German Dadaists created out of nihilism and chaos.

While such heads as nos AI. 21-25 are undoubtedly expressive, their cavities and overlapping features recall the mutilated Greek carvings in the

Glyptothek, Munich, where Paolozzi has regularly spent his Sunda drawing. They can readily be seen as ancient harbingers of Cubist sculptur The fragmented and sliced heads of gods and heroes in the Munich museu are literally two millennia-old survivors of the destruction-creation parado This gives them an added layer of meaning for Paolozzi who described h own use of time when making the collage for the screenprint **Wittgenste in New York** of 1964 (C3.7) as 'being manipulated, so that some of th images are separated by thirty years of yellowing in portfolios, waiting for th day'.[3]

Distortions not dissimilar to those of the portrait sculptures can also t found in a series of **Heads** made in 1978-9 (A3.9-14). Their feathe drypoint lines describe machine elements superimposed on blurre anatomies which were drawn with a pantograph – a draughtsma instrument for copying drawings in different scales.

The same principle of dissection and reassembly underpinning the rece portrait heads also informed the very first 'machine' head of 195 **Mr Cruikshank** (AI.2), which is based on a sectionalised wooden mod made by the Massachusetts Institute of Technology to measure irradiatic on the human skull. Reminiscent of Dada objects of the 1920s, its hypnot stare resembles the robotic heroine of the expressionist film **Metropoli** who also figures in one of Paolozzi's silkscreen prints in the series **Gener Dynamic Fun** of 1970 (C3.16).

'Divine ambiguity is possible with collage: flesh marred by object or obje masquerading as flesh. There is nothing astonishing in that; witness the gre portraits of Arcimboldo. We have also learned to define collage as a proce where dreams can be rejected and the victims exposed to ridicule'.[4]

At about the time that Paolozzi projected popular images in h Independent Group lecture called 'BUNK', given at the Institute Contemporary Arts in 1952, and which influenced the course of Pop art Britain, he also made a number of collaged portraits, based on **Tim** magazine covers of world leaders, industrialists and film stars. Like the rece sculpture, they consist of ready-made features cut up and recombined collage to make new imaginary heroes. They have not been exhibited

Left: Glyptothek, Munich

Centre: 'Whose Afraid of Sugar Pink and Lime Green', 1971

Right: **Camera**, 1979

ublic for thirty years but like the seminal 'BUNK' images, possess ironic wit their reflections on men and women in power.[5]

On an anthropomorphic level, the heads of the 1950s encrusted with heir civilization's detritus, like **Krokodeel** (A1.6) carry human references; nd human heads of the same period have animal associations.

The head, whether by a Greek or an African artist, has an even more ompelling presence when overlaid in collage by a twentieth-century nachine image. In early collages of the 1940s, machine parts are uperimposed on images of Greek sculpture (A2.6); and scrapbooks of the 950s and 1960s contain numerous collages of a similar kind. In an ironic eference to the making of modern sculpture, juxtapositions are made by ringing machine elements into direct contact with plates from a 1920s culptor's manual,[6] which Paolozzi would have been advised to study as a culpture student at the Slade School of Art in 1945 (A2.5).

The other group of recent sculpture consists of a series of machine heads ulminating in the large cast-iron sculpture **Piscator** of 1980-81, made for uston Square, London. These heads were originally conceived from a eady-made which Paolozzi described in 1979 as being 'slightly African, vhich I quite like . . . the bottom part is based on a motor-bike, but the top art is an invention'.[7]

The relationship of the lower 'ready-made' element to the upper nvention' echoes the 1960 **Collage over African Sculpture** which in its urn recalls the interest Paolozzi took in African sculpture at the Pitt Rivers Museum, Oxford, while studying at the Slade in 1945 (A2.3), and the Picasso-like rephrasing of African sculpture in the gouache and collage **Head** of 1947.

The top 'invention' of the machine heads was developed from graphic magery relating to the **Calcium Light Night** screenprints of 1974-6 C3.26-34) and to the reliefs of the mid-1970's (B1.7-13). It was leveloped, with expansive elaborations, in two major sculpture commis-ions: **Hommage à Bruckner**, 1977, in Linz, Austria; and **Camera**, 1978-9, or the Munich Patent Office.

NOTES

1. Eduardo Paolozzi, 'Collage or a Scenario for a Comedy of Critical Hallucination' in **Eduardo Paolozzi, Collages and Drawings**, Anthony d'Offay, London 23 March – 22 April 1977 (exhibition catalogue).

2. **Eduardo Paolozzi**, BBC, Radio 3, March 1984.

3. Frank Whitford, 'Paolozzi', **Art and Design BBC Radiovision**, 1971, p. 8.

4. Eduardo Paolozzi, 'Collage or a Scenario for a Comedy of Critical Hallucination', 1977.

5. **Collages and Objects**, (Exhibition organised by Lawrence Alloway), Institute of Contemporary Arts, 13 October – 20 November 1954 (Cat. nos. 46-49). The previous year the ICA held an exhibition devoted to the symbolism of the head in mythology, pre-history and art. 'Wonder and Horror of the Human Head', 6 March – 19 April 1953; introduction by Herbert Read and Roland Penrose. Sections included 'Sun and Moon', 'Head as Creative Force', 'Devouring Head', 'The Head and Death', 'Multiple Heads', 'Geometric Form', 'Distortion', 'Expression', 'Meta-morphosis', 'Caricature', 'Bird and Animal', and works and reproductions by Dürer, Klee, Brancusi, Ernst and Magritte. The exhibition also included a section devoted to representations of the head in popular art and advertising, planned by Lee Miller.

6. Albert Toft, **Modelling and Sculpture**, London 1929.

7. Eduardo Paolozzi, **The Development of the Idea**, Crawford Centre for the Arts, University of St Andrews, 11 May – 9 June, 1979 (exhibition catalogue).

AI.4

AI

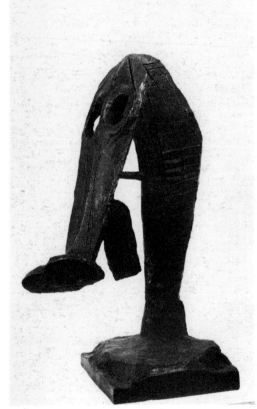

AI.1

AI.I Horse's Head
Bronze, 1946
Edition of 3, 1974
47.5 × 28.5 × 26.2
City of Edinburgh Museums and Galleries
Exh: London 1947; Hannover 1974-5 (1: repr. p. 56);
A.C.G.B. 1976-7 (1: repr. p. 9)
Lit: R. Melville 'Eduardo Paolozzi' Horizon XVI Sept. 1947
p. 213 repr. pp. 212; Konnertz 1984 p. 26 repr. pls. 35,
36.
Melville reproduces 2 versions of the original; one in white
concrete, a second version in red concrete (whereabouts
unknown). One was probably exhibited at the Mayor Gallery,
London, 1947.

AI.2 Mr Cruikshank
Bronze, 1950
Edition of 9
28 × 28 × 20
City of Edinburgh Museums and Galleries
Exh: London 1971 (30); Hanover 1974-5 (5: repr. p. 65);
A.C.G.B. 1976-7 (4: repr.)
See Plate X

AI.3 Head
Bronze, c. 1954
27 × 36 × 18.5
Lit: Sotheby's 1983 (280) repr.
Originally a gift from the artist to the architects Maxwell Fry
and Jane Drew.

AI.4 Shattered Head
Bronze, 1956
Edition of 6
28.5 × 24.2 × 18.5

The Tate Gallery
Exh: London 1958 (36: repr); Hanover 1974-5 (8: rep
p. 69); Berlin 1975 (15: repr. p. 77)
Lit: Kirkpatrick 1970 p. 35 repr. pl. 26; Konnertz 1984 pp. 82
5, 87, 270 repr. pl. 161
A related ink drawing dated 1955 was exhibited in Hanove
1974-5 (47: repr. p. 68). The brutalized, grotesque imager
of this head is also explored in sculptured figures of the perio
such as **Damaged Warrior** (AI.5)

AI.5 Damaged Warrior
Bronze, s 'E.Paolozzi', 1956
26.5 × 14 × 15.2
Exh. London 1958 (37: repr.); London 1971 (35); Hanove
1974-5 (6: repr. p. 70)
Lit: Kirkpatrick 1970 p. 35 repr. pl. 23; Konnertz 198
pl. 87
A similar sculpture entitled **Little Warrior**, 1956, was also fir
exhibited at the Hanover Gallery, London in 1958 (34
repr.)

AI.6 Krokodeel
Bronze, 1956
94 × 60 × 20
Private Colection
Exh: Hanover 1974-5 (9: repr. p. 78); Berlin 1975 (16: rep
p. 86)
Lit: Tate 1971 repr. p. 68; Konnertz 1984 pp. 87,91 rep
pl. 172
One of a series of heads of the mid-1950s (see also **AG.**
AI.7) made by the lost wax process. Translating the theme
the **Automobile Head** collage of 1954 into sculptur
Paolozzi used found objects to create the complex surface
which give these heads their facial 'expressions'.
See Plate X

HEADS AND PORTRAIT

.7 **AG5**

onze, 1958

1.6 × 83.8 × 38

ivate collection

h: Hanover 1974-5 (14: repr. p. 79); Berlin 1975 (24:
pr. p. 87);

: Konnertz 1984 pp. 87,91 repr. pl. 174

.5

AI.7

AI.8

AI.10

AI.11

AI.12

HEADS AND PORTRAI⸛

Small Portrait
ze, 1977
n of 6
× 13.5 × 5.5
St Andrews 1979 (56); Edinburgh 1979 (172) repr.
Cologne 1979 repr. p. 42.

Portrait of Matta
ze, s 'E.Paolozzi', 1978
20 8.5
St Andrews 1979 (57); Edinburgh 1979 (exc. cat);
gne 1979 (repr. p. 42)
onnert 1984 p. 240, 241, repr. pl. 439
late IX for a reproduction of the wax version.

AI.10 **Naked Head**
Bronze, 1978
39 × 35 × 14.5
Collection of the Royal Academy
Exh: St Andrews 1979 (58) repr.
Lit: Konnertz 1984 pp. 240,241 repr. pl. 436

AI.11 **Naked Head II**
Bronze sd 'E Paolozzi 78'
35 × 35.5 × 13.5
City of Edinburgh Museums and Galleries

AI.12 **Large Head**
Bronze, 1979
43.2 × 84 × 40.75
Lit: Konnertz 1984 pp. 240, 241 repr. pl. 438

AI.13 **Head Looking Up**
Bronze, 1980
36 × 15 × 27
Lit: Konnertz 1984 pp. 241 repr. pl. 441
Of the bronze heads of this period this one is most closely
related to the large cast iron sculpture, **Piscator** 1980-81,
situated in Euston Square, London.
See Plate 11

AI.14 **Small Head**
Plaster, 1980
10.5 × 6.5 × 4.5

AI.14

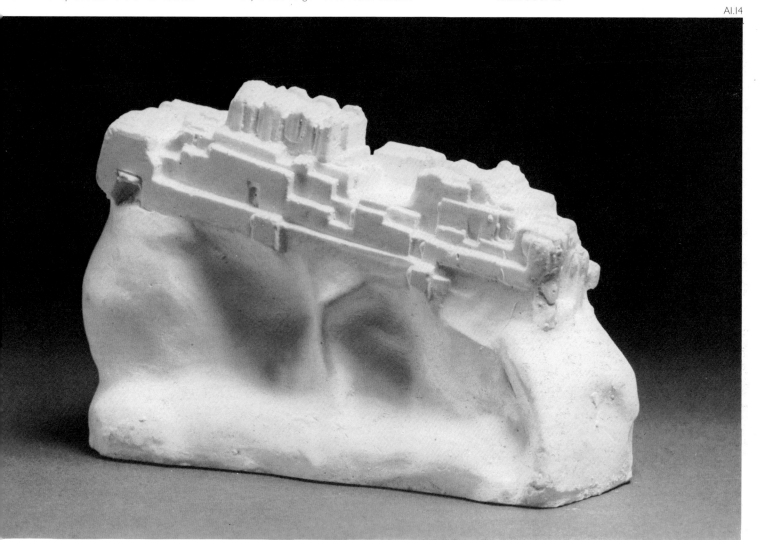

AI.15 **Head**
Wax, 1983/4
34 x 20 x 17

AI.16 **Head**
Wax, 1983/4
32 x 18 x 16

AI.17 **Head**
Plaster, 1983/4
33 x 15.5 x 25

AI.15

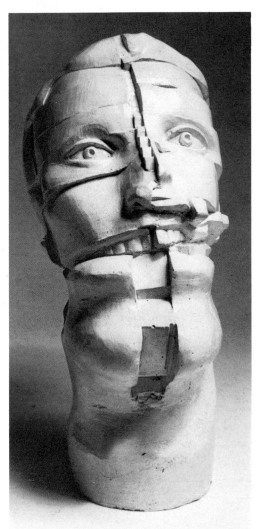

AI.16

AI.17

HEADS AND PORTR

20

AI.19

AI.21 Electric Bishop
Painted plaster and rope, 1984
40 x 31 x 22.5cm
See front cover

AI.22 Head
Bronze, 1982
Edition of 3, different patina on each
30 x 15.5 x 18
Collection: The Minories, Essex
Lit: Konnertz 1984 p. 270 repr. pl. 277
See Plate X

AI.23 Portrait of an Actor (for Luis Bunuel)
Bronze, 1984
35 x 27.5 x 19.5cm
Lit: Royal Academy Summer Exhibition Illustrated Catalogue
1984
See Plate V

AI.24 Yukio Mishima
Bronze, 1984
See Plate I

AI.25 Walk Man Study
Bronze on painted wood base, 1984
40.5 cx 17.25 x 20.25cm
See Plate X

AI.26 Untitled
Bronze, 1983
Edition of 2
36 x 15.25 x 15.75

AI.27 Untitled
Bronze, 1984
Edition of 2
38.5 x 20.5 x 17.25 cm

28

AI.26

A2.12

A2.8

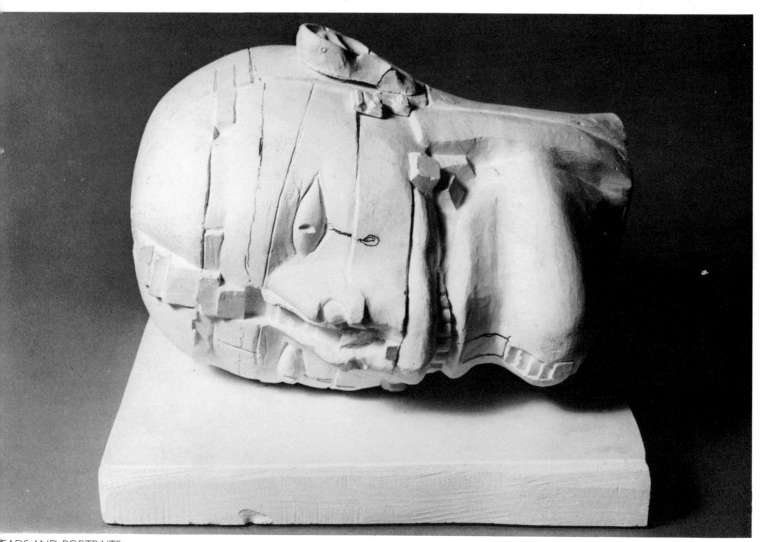

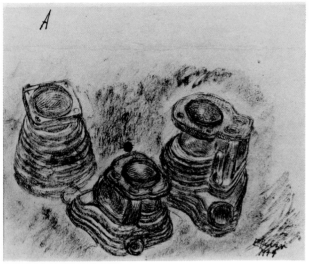

A2.1

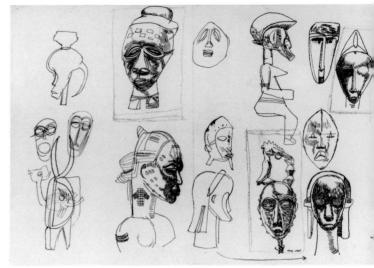

A2.3

A2.1 **Engine Head**
Pencil and ink on card, 1944
23 × 28.5
Lit: Cleveland 6th International Drawing Biennale p. 10 repr.
p. 19

A2.2 **Drawings after Rembrandt**
Inscribed 'copies from Rembrandt Ashmolean Museum
Oxford 1945 Eduardo Paolozzi'.
Ink
24.5 × 35.5
Private Collection
Exh: London 1971 (3: repr. fig. 1); Hanover 1974-5 (35: repr.
p. 54); Berlin 1975 (81: repr. pl. 54); London 1977
(203)
Lit: Konnertz 1984 p. 22 repr. pl. 27.
Made whilst Paolozzi was at the Slade School of Art, evacuated
to Oxford in wartime. Another page of drawings after
Rembrandt is reproduced in Konnertz 1984 pl. 28.

A2.3 **Drawings after African Sculpture**
Ink, 1945
38.4 × 56.6
Arts Council of Great Britain
Exh: London 1971 (1)
Lit: Konnertz 1984 p. 22 repr. pl. 29.
Drawings made after African Sculpture in the Pitt Rivers
Museum, Oxford, when Paolozzi was studying at the Slade
School in 1945.

A2.2

4 Marchese Marconi
llage sd 'E Paolozzi 1946'
5 × 13

6 Head of Zeus
lage, sd 'E Paolozzi 1946'
× 17.5

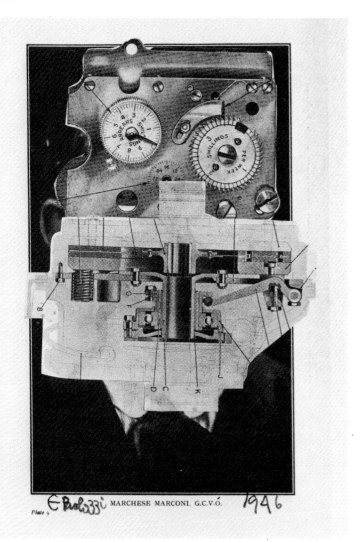

MARCHESE MARCONI. G.C.V.O.   1946

7. Head of Zeus. From the pediment on Pl. 1.
Athens, Acropolis Museum. P. 20.

BUST PEG SHOWING "BUTTERFLY" SUSPENDED BY A PIECE
OF WIRE FROM WHERE COMPO PIPES CROSS OVER
ONE ANOTHER

Note piece of wood to carry shoulders. From this, "butterflies" can be
suspended when thought necessary.

A2.5 **Butterfly**
Collage sd '1946 E Paolozzi'
19.7 x 13.6
Lit: Konnertz 1984 p. 29 repr. pl. 46
Part of the image is derived from an illustration in 'Mode
and Sculpture' by Albert Toft.

2.7 **Self Portrait**
collage, sd 'E Paolozzi 1947'
8 × 25.5

2.8 **Juice King**
collage, sd 'E Paolozzi 1948'
7.5 × 24.5
ee Plate VI

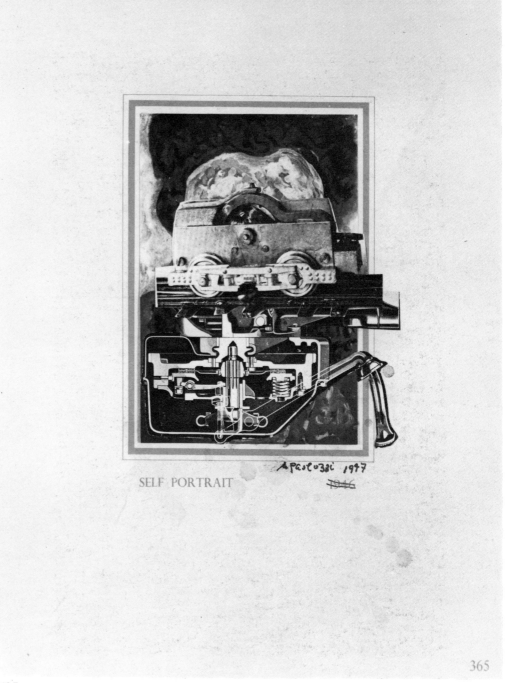

SELF PORTRAIT

365

A2.7

A2.9 Star Kist
Collage, sd 'E Paolozzi 1948'
36 x 24

A2.10 7-Up
Collage, sd 'E Paolozzi 1949'
40.25 x 27.5

A2.11 Real Gold
Collage, sd 'E Paolozzi 1949'
28.25 x 41
Part of the image is similar to that used in one of the 'Bunk'
collages of 1950 also entitled **Real Gold**.

A2.12 Life Savers
Collage, sd 'E Paolozzi 49'
37.5 x 24
See Plate VI

A2.11

A2.9

A2.10

HEADS AND PORTRAIT

2.13 **From Puckers to Puccini, and Mozart too**
ollage, 1952
3 × 21
ee Plate VII

2.14 **We Dare Once More**
ollage, 1952
4 × 21
ee Plate VII

A2.15 **One Party in Three Parts**
Collage, 1952
26.25 × 21.5

A2.16 **A New Look**
Collage, 1952
20.5 × 21.25cm

A2.17 **No Easter without Good Friday**
Collage, 1952
25.25 × 18.5

2.15

A2.16

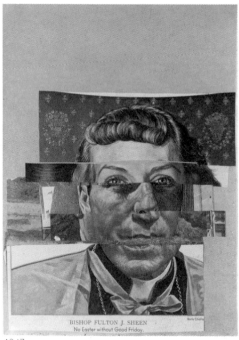

A2.17

A2.18

A2.18 **One Man Track Team**
Collage, 1952
27.25 × 20.75

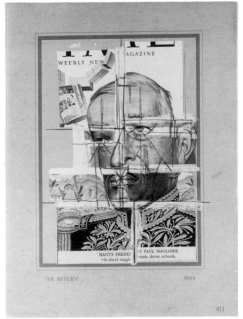

A2.19

A2.19 **The Return**
Collage, 1952
33 × 25.5

A2.21

A2.21 **To Rule is to Take Orders**
Collage, 1952
22.75 × 15.5

A2.22 **From Mass Merchandising Profit**
Collage, 1952
35 × 22.75

A2.22

A2.23 **North of the Border**
Collage, 1952
33.25 × 25.5

A2.23

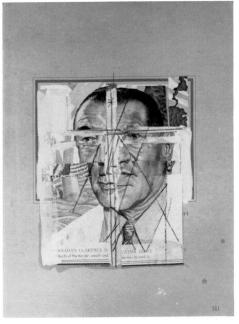

A2.24 **Children of the Night**
Collage, 1952
33.25 × 25.25

A2.24

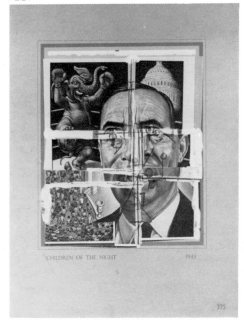

20 **Keep it Simple, Keep it Sexy, Keep it Sad**
lage, 1952
25 × 21.5

A2.20

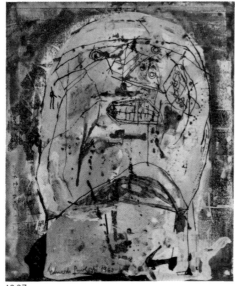

A2.27

A2.25 **Head II**
Collage, ink and oil, 1953
55 x 36
The British Council

A2.26 **Head III**
Monotype, sd 'Eduardo Paolozzi 1953'
56 x 43
The British Council
Lit: Kirkpatrick 1970 p. 27 repr. pl. 15

A2.27 **Head**
Ink and gouache on paper, 1953
43.5 x 38.5 inches
Property of a Gentleman

A2.25

A2.26

HEADS AND PORTRA

A2.29

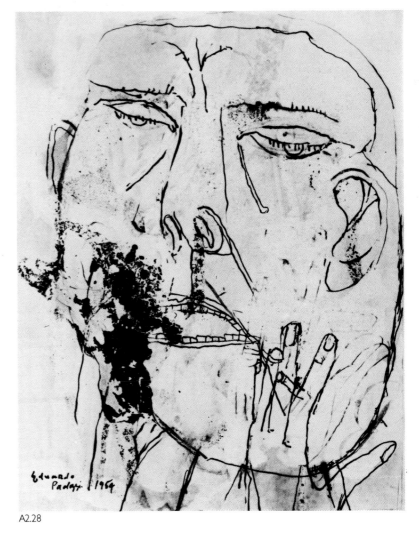

A2.28

A2.30 **Paper Head**
Paper, sd 'E.P.1980'
49 × 31
Exh: Oxford 1982 (repr. p. 23)
Lit: Paolozzi 1983 p. 42 repr. fig. 7
'Like an African mask, the Head is a fusion of man and machine which has appeared over the years in both my graphics and sculpture. For this object pulp is made from old rags with a home-made Hollander. It is then spooned into a negative mould, the positive having been modelled from a drypoint.' (E. Paolozzi in 'Innovations in Contemporary Printmaking', Oxford 1982 p. 21).

A2.31 **Warrior's Head**
Pencil on paper, 1982
32.5 × 24

A2.32 **Self Portrait**
'Charles of the Ritz' make-up on paper, 1983
46 × 36
Zeev Aram

METROPOLITAN OPERA'S PATRICE MUNSEL
From puckers to Puccini, and Mozart, too.

"We must dare once more and do better."

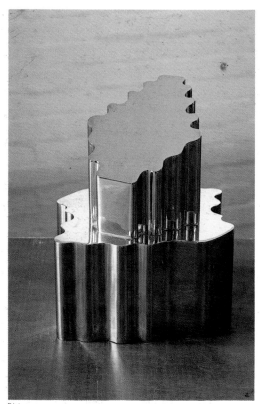

B1.1

A3.16

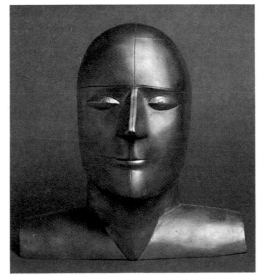

AI.2

AI.6

AI.25

AI.22

A 1st point
B 2nd
C 3rd point
D 4
E 5

Munich EPaolozzi 1982

A2.31

A3.2

A3.1

A3.1 **Never Leave Well Enough Alone**
Lithograph, 1972
26.75 × 36.5
Lit: London 1977 (128)
From the 'Bunk' series, material which Paolozzi collected in Paris and London between 1947-52, collaged and subsequently facsimilied by lithograph and screenprint in 1972. The title of this particular print is that of the autobiography of the industrial designer Raymond Loewy (pub. New York 1951). 'Bunk' was the title of Paolozzi's lecture given to the Independent Group at the ICA in the Summer of 1952.

A3.2 **Man Holds the Key**
Screenprint, 1972
34 × 23
Lit: London 1977 (130)

A3.3 **Windtunnel Test**
Screeprint and lithograph, 1972
38.8 × 26
Lit: London 1977 (124) Konnertz 1984 repr. pl. 365
From the series 'Bunk'. Printed in 1972 from the original collage of 1950.

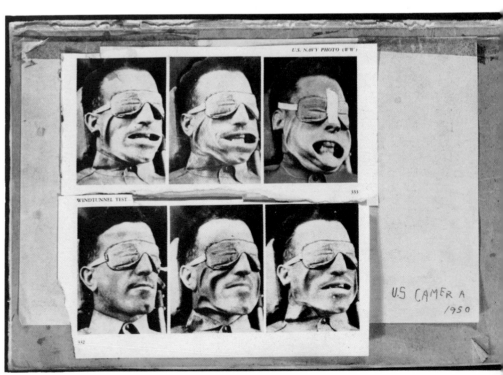

A3.3

3.4 Automobile Head

reenprint, 1954

x 33

he British Council

t: Middleton 1963 repr; Reichardt 1963 repr. p. 79; hneede 1970 repr. p. 5; Kirkpatrick 1970 pp. 29, 35 repr. 18; Whitford 1971 p. 13 repr. p. 12; London 1971 repr. 20a; Konnertz 1984 pp. 81, 82, 87, 91, 110, 158, 165, 271, pr. pl. 152

ne of a number of silkscreen editions after an original collage 1954 (editions in 1954, 1957, 1958, 1962, 1963 and 1980). example of Paolozzi's form of Brutalism which appears also his sculpture of the 1950s. The interplay of mechanical and uman forms emerges as an underlying theme through much his work. Here various engine parts conform with atomical features such as the engine 'brain' and the ankshaft 'spine'. In later variations, machine elements are xpressive of facial features (e.g. **Hero as a Riddle**, 1963, .5)

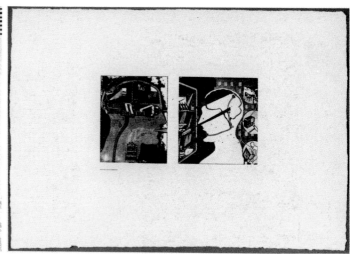

A3.6

A3.8

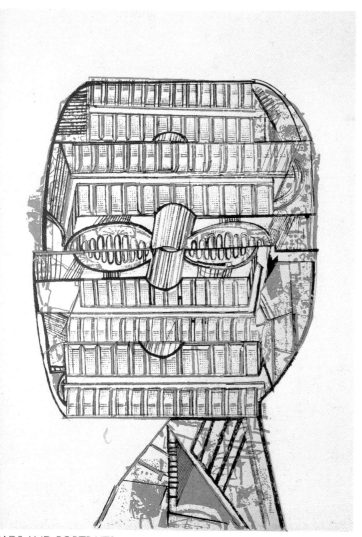

A3.7

A3.5 **Hero As A Riddle**   A3.4
Screenprint, 1953
Edition of 10
91 × 58/66 × 44
Lit: London 1977 (15)

A3.6 **The Silken World of Michelangelo**
Screenprint, 1967
38 × 25.5
Lit: Kirkpatrick 1970, pp. 98, 102, 110-11, 114, 133; London
1977 (37); Konnertz 1984 pp. 171ff. 178 repr. p. 1325
From the **Moonstrips Empire News** series of 1967.
A3.9

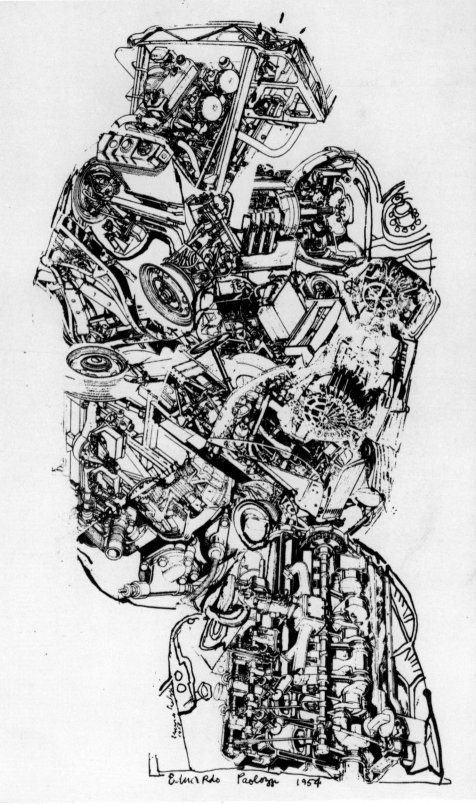

7 **Inside the Brain**
togravure, 1970
5 × 39.5/20.4 × 13.9
Konnertz 1984 pp. 64, 101, 170, 186, 188ff, 192
m the **Conditional Probability Machine** series of
0.

3 **Perception Through Impression**
tgravure, 1970
5 × 39.5/19.1 × 30.4
London 1977 (63); Konnertz 1984 pp. 64, 101, 170, 186,
ff, 192 repr. pl. 347
m the **Conditional Probability Machine** series of
0.

9 **Head**
ing, 1977
× 27.5/33.25 × 17.5

A3.10 **Head**
Etching, 1979
68 × 50/45 × 30

A3.11 **Head**
Etching, 1979
68 × 50/45 × 30

A3.12 **Head**
Etching, 1979
57 × 38.5/45.5 × 30.5

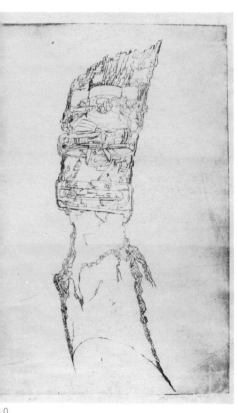

0

A3.11

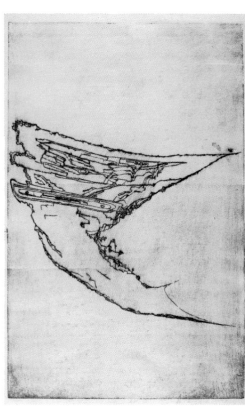

A3.12

A3.13 Head
Etching, 1979
68 × 50/45.5 × 30

A3.14 Head
58 × 39.5/45.5 × 30

A3.15 Head
Etching, 1980
58 × 38.5/45.15 × 30.25

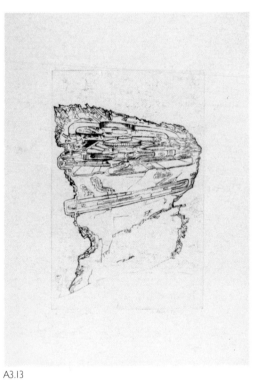

A3.13

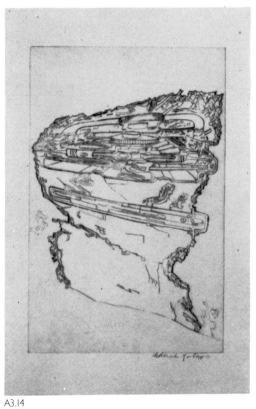

A3.14

A3.15

HEADS AND PORTRA

6 **A New Spirit In Painting**
ographic silkscreen, 1982-3
x 65
title refers to the Royal Academy of Arts Exhibition of
, the fiscal and aesthetic implications of which Paolozzi
rously opposed.
Plate VIII

7 **Beetle Head**
hing, 1984
5 x 51/39 x 29.25
ion of 5
A3.17-19 were all made at Chelsea School of Art, April/
1984.

8 **Beetle II**
hing, 1984
ion of 5
5 x 51/39 x 29

A3.17

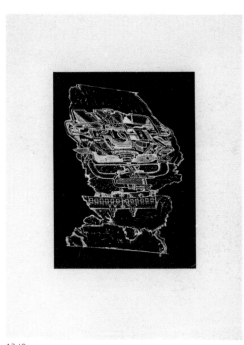

A3.18

A3.20 **Head I**
Woodcut, 1984
57 × 38

A3.21 **Head III**
Woodcut, 1984
57 × 38

A3.22 **Dumont Head**
Etching, 1984
23.5 × 15.5/29 × 23

A3.22

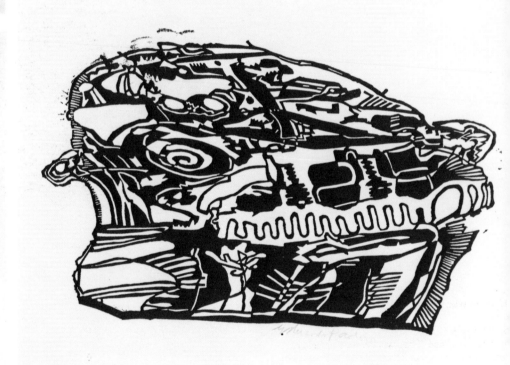

A3.20

.19 **Head** (von Prinzhorn)

:hing,

5 x 51/34.74 x 22.75 Edition of 5

ns Prinzhorn (1886-1933) was the author of a study on

e art of the insane (publ. Berlin 1922).

A3.19

A3.23 **Now here is the News**
Etching, 1984
50.5 × 57.25/23.15 × 31.25

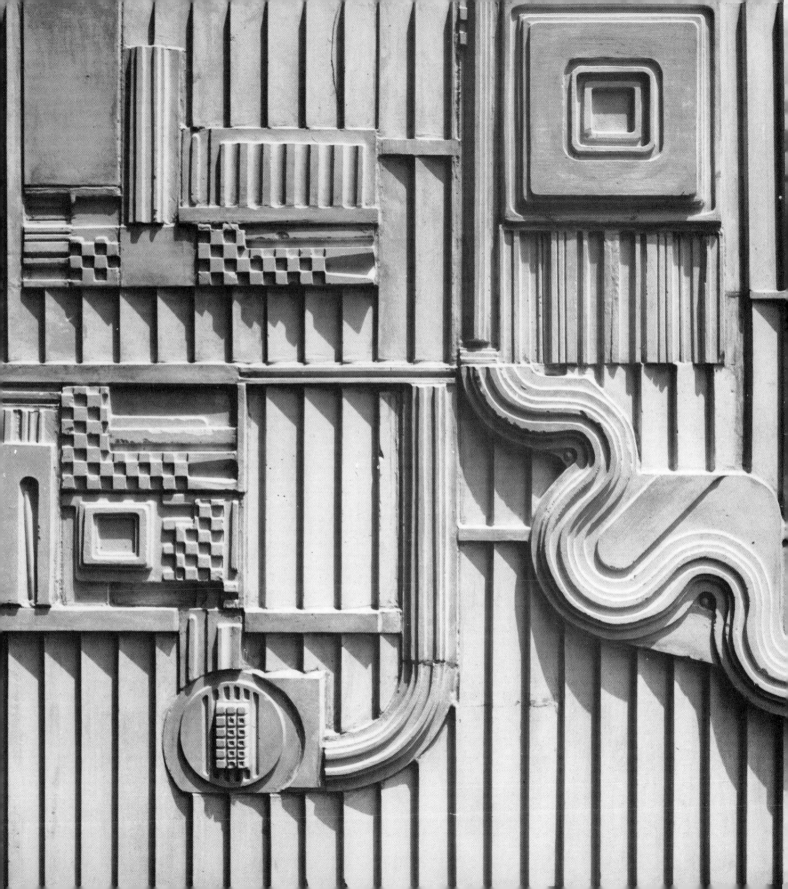

From 'Cleish' to 'Clock': Landscape in Relief

The design sheets: a world within a world. A landscape within a face. A ridge and three mountains suggest a smile.

Eduardo Paolozzi, c. 1958.

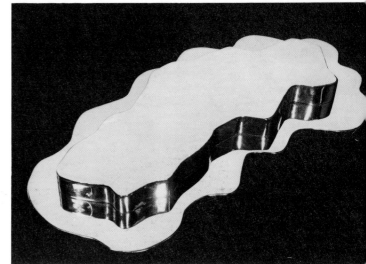
Aril, 1966   Earl

Paolozzi has now done more than any other artist, painter or sculptor, to re-establish the relief as a medium for modern art. At the end of the nineteenth century the bas-relief had little to offer sculptors: this in spite of, but paradoxically because of, Rodin's domination in the medium with his great **Portes d'Enfer**, out of which he developed a lifetime's vocabulary of forms for both sculptures and graphic art.

Rodin's example was not lost on Paolozzi, living in Paris in 1947, for he admired – and still holds in awe – the wealth of imagery and symbolist expression in Rodin's sculpture. After Picasso had made pictures with papiers collées and collage, and sculptures from cardboard and tin, the doors were open for the Surrealists (such as Arp and Giacometti whom Paolozzi knew at this time) who did not make distinctions between one medium and the other. Paintings were encrusted with plaster or sand and given textured surfaces, like Masson's, Max Ernst's or Dubuffet's; and several of Arp's wooden sculptured objects were painted in bright colours. But in England, not since Arp gave Ben Nicholson the idea of making wood and plaster reliefs conceived in a pictorial format in the 1930s has the sculptural potential of relief been so fully tested and explored.

Paolozzi first made reliefs in 1947-8, during his Paris period, some three years before he made a screenprint. They consist of insects, leaves and aquatic imagery pressed into clay and cast in wax or plaster: none seem to have been taken beyond the plaster stage.

The technique of impressing found objects into wax and then making a cast in plaster was integral to the process Paolozzi used to create his figure sculptures in the 1950s (A1.1-3). So while the landscape convention of the relief disappeared from his work for nearly twenty years, its collage principle lived on to serve the expressionist surfaces of his three-dimensional robotic sculpture, the engineered aluminium sculpture of the 1960s, and the decorative symbolism of the screenprints.

In 1958 Paolozzi made the contribution of the relief to his art very clear in a text called 'Metamorphosis of Rubbish' in which he listed 'objects which are used in my work, that is to say, pressed into a slab of clay in different formations. This forms an exact impression (in the negative, of course) and

from this a store of design sheets can be built up. They range from extrem mechanical shapes to resembling pieces of bark'. He stated that his cur obsession was 'with metamorphosis of the figure', but implied that principle of relief was still capable of modern expression, of the k paralleled by the ancient archaeological language of Egyptian hieroglyp

The reliefs, from **Cleish**, 1971 (B1.3-6), to **Clock**, 1984, (B1.24 period of some fourteen years, look different from previous work. They not so much metaphoric, but may better be described as synaesthetic. Th to say they evoke and configure senses in addition to sight, such as music sound. Many of them share their imagery with the series of screenpri **Calcium Light Night**, 1974-6 (C3.26-34), which are dedicated to American composer Charles Ives. The reliefs seem more formal than work, classical even, just as detailed as before, but with the detail distilled refined into geometric metaphors which are open to interpretations much sensory as intellectual. More recently, the sense of touch is explore reliefs with movable parts for blind children, **Rhino** (B1.22) and **PIAN** (B1.23), which is dedicated to Louise Nevelson and Sophie-Taeuber Arp whom Paolozzi is personally drawn in friendship and in obvious art affinity.

It was not until 1971 that the landscape convention of the square rectangular relief reappeared in Paolozzi's sculpture. Only in part was reaction against the colourful figurative imagery of the screenprints, and space-occupying sculpture of the previous decade. More importantl

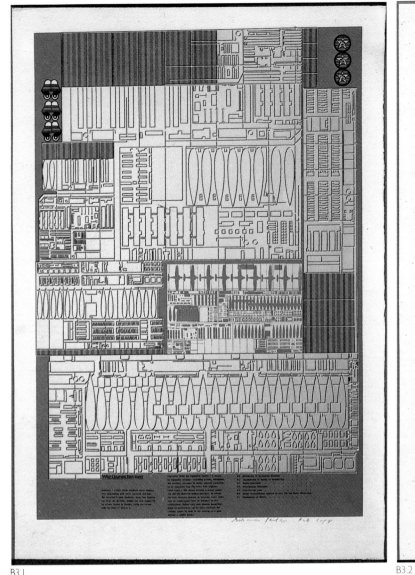

B3.1

B3.2

g design

Cleish ceiling (B2.8-11) redevelop the graphic themes which had been left off some twenty years before. They are another example of what Paolozzi has described as 'parts of an experience which is previous work pressing through'.[4]

Because the relief evokes the association and feeling of a landscape it is not surprising that Paolozzi should have gone on to make landscape prints and drawings. In an interview in 1979 he said:

'I'm doing some prints on the Landscape, but in my case it's six variations on the Parking Space . . . That's how I treat the history of art: as I see it, in my way, and they've all got mechanical connotations'.[5]

The subject of landscape made its appearance in several of the Ernst-like collages of 1949 and resurfaced in the 1960 film Paolozzi made, **The History of Nothing**. Several of the highly polished chrome sculptues of 1967, such as **Aril** gave free standing form to the relief. Their waving contours appear to have been developed out of the fecund graphic imagery of the **As is When** screenprints of the mid-1960s (C3.2-14). More recently, a number of landscaping etchings include uniquely collaged staffage – animals, motor vehicles etc. – to indicate the type and mood of landscape depicted: for example **Parkplatz** (D3.14-15).

For his reliefs Paolozzi has built up a repertoire of the simplest elements, fretsawed out of thrown-away wood rescued from skips, often the one stationed outside the back door of the Royal College of Art. The process is similar to the way he used the vocabulary of machine parts made up for him by the engineering works where he made aluminium sculpture in the 1960s, but the method has more of the 'hand-made' look than that of the machine. Although the individual pieces look simple in themselves, they build up to make much more complex visual statements. As the viewer moves from one side of a relief to the other, scans its surface up and down, the peaks and troughs built up from the surface create new viewpoints and new meanings through multiple perspectives. This constantly shifting visual experience is integral to Paolozzi's sculpture, as to his prints. The reliefs are a bridge between the prints and the sculpture. When he came to make the reliefs for the cast aluminium doors for the entrance to the Hunterian Museum at Glasgow University, he used a technique of building up the collaged plaster elements onto boards which he had previously used for cutting up slivers of his screenprints to make etchings. 'It is a kind of freedom', he has explained, 'to shuffle between the two worlds of printmaking and sculpture'.[6]

sented the opportunity of examining again the formal properties of ture-making that had begun with relief nearly thirty years before.

There are very few of Paolozzi's abstract drawings in this period which do carry a hint of three-dimensional depth. It can be expressed by the angle ough which a line turns, or by the weight and shading of graphic marks their relationship one to another. Once the pictorial language had been ablished – it derives from an abstract visualisation of organ music made by erman artist in the 1920s (repr. Konnertz fig. 369) – it could be made to ve both sculpture and graphics. Many of the drawings of the 1970s are y beautiful in their own right. Some evoke the cobwebbed structure of asso's analytical figure subjects of 1910; others are haunted by the fading sence of the metamorphic figures which filled the prints and informed the lptural imagery of ten years before.

Historically a relief has its origins in picture-making as much as in sculpture. cient Assyrian reliefs and classical sculptures were often coloured; and ently Paolozzi has reintroduced colour into his wood relief, in **Clock**, .24), as he did in some of his aluminium sculptures twenty years .[2]

The fact that the length and breadth of a relief generally exceeds its depth ans that it can be looked down on from above, as well as hung on a wall. us it can be made to resemble a ground plan or architectural cityscape, h as that of Frank Lloyd Wright's Broadacre City, to which Paolozzi also ers in the series of **Utopia** prints (D3.25-6) which are dedicated to the nerican architect. A not dissimilar language was invented in woodcut for ght's spiritual brother from Scotland, Charles Rennie Mackintosh.

Looking down on a relief mirrors the actual process of its making, for it is vitably laid on a floor or table while the modelled elements are moved und. Conversely, the first work in the series being for a ceiling at Cleish stle, it follows, if exceptionally, that a relief can also be viewed from below. lozzi first made a ceiling decoration in 1952 when he screenprinted a ck design on white paper for one of Sir Ove Arup's offices.[3] The design is ilar to several Schwitters-like collage and gouaches made at this time, in ich vertical and horizontal geometry predominate. The drawings for the

Notes

1. Eduardo Paolozzi, 'Metamorphosis of Rubbish', 'Notes from a Lecture at the Institute of Contemporary Arts', **Uppercase** no. 1, 1958. Reprinted in Diane Kirkpatrick, **Eduardo Paolozzi**, London 1970, pp 120-130.

2. Richard Hamilton, interview with Eduardo Paolozzi, **Arts Yearbook** 8, 1965. Reprinted in **Eduardo Paolozzi, Sculpture, Drawings, Collages and Graphics**, Arts Council exhibition, 1976-77, pp. 35-40.

3. A collage mural of 1962 for the office of Fry, Drew and Partners, is reproduced in Kirkpatrick, op.cit., plate 29.

4 Eduardo Paolozzi, BBC, Radio 3, March 1984.

5. Eduardo Paolozzi, **The Development of the Idea**, Crawford Centre for the Arts, University of St Andrews, 11 May-9 June 1979.

6. Eduardo Paolozzi, 'Where Reality Lies', **The Oxford Art Journal**, vol. 6, no.1, 1983, p. 44.

BI.1 Untitled
Chromed steel, c. 1967
62 × 92 × 55

BI.2 Untitled
Polished bronze, 1968-9
15 × 30 × 23.5
See Plate VIII

BI.3 Small Study for Cleish Ceiling
Wood, 1972
84.5 × 83.5 × 6.4
Exh. London 1976 (6, repr. p. 9); A.C.G.B. 1976-77 (13, repr. p. 51); St Andrews 1979 (48); Edinburgh 1979 (65)
Lit. Cologne 1979 repr. p. 48

BI.4 Small Study for Cleish Ceiling
Wood, painted white, 1972
33.5 × 23.5 × 4.5
Exh. Berlin 1975 (68; London 1976 (9)

BI.5 Study for Cleish Ceiling
Wood, 1973
172 × 173.5 × 6.5
Exh. Berlin 1975 (70, repr. p. 129); London 1976 (10, repr. p. 10); Edinburgh 1976 (5)
Lit. Konnertz 1984 pp. 205, 214, 216, 227, 269, repr. pl. 386, 388, 389
See Plate XIII

BI.6 Study for Cleish Ceiling
Resin, aluminium-coloured finished panel, 1973
172 × 173.5 × 6.5
The finished panels, cast in resin and aluminium-colour were commissioned by the architect Michael Spens for Cl Castle, Kinross. They were designed to fill nine recessed a in the ceiling of the main sitting-room and were com mented by three tapestry blinds, also designed by Paolozzi a large adjacent window. Unfortunately both the panels tapestries were removed when the castle was sold. inspiration for these designs and for several other wo (e.g. **Kosmos**, 1970, B3.4) came from a reproduction c German abstract painting of the 1920s, interpreting or music.
For reproductions of the panels and tapestries **in situ** London 1976 p. 6, London 1984, p. 12 and Konnertz 1 pl. 385.

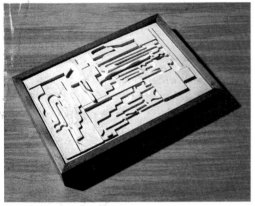

BI.4

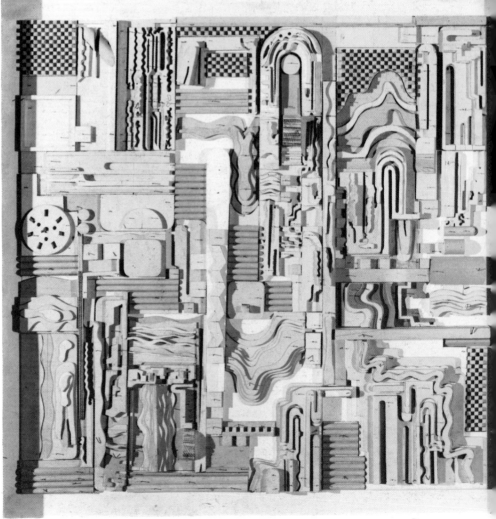

BI.3

BI.8

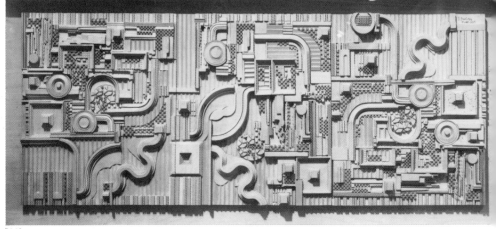

BI.10

BI.7 **Moniz**
Wood, 1975
45 x 19 x 3.8
Exh. London 1976 (12); A.C.G.B. 1976-7 (18, repr. p. 52)

BI.8 **S.I.G.N.**
Wood, 1975
68 x 28.5 x 4.5
Exh. London 1976 (13, repr. p. 15)
The repetition of the same design, in **Moniz** and **S.I.G.N.**, in a different scale, illustrates the way size influences perception.

BI.9 **Proxmira**
Wood, 1975
38 x 14.5 x 3.8
Exh. London 1976 (14, repr. p. 15)
See Plate XIV

BI.10 **Study for Niigata-Turkoma**
Wood, 1975
61 x 152.5 x 5
Exh. London 1976 (6)
As well as a bronze version (BI.11) the relief was also ca resin: see London 1976 (26, repr. p. 17) and Edinburgh I (14).

BI.11

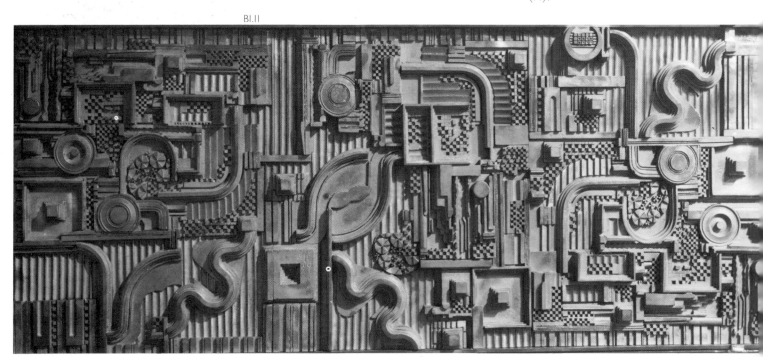

FROM CLEISH TO CLO

Niigata-Turkoma

ze, 1975

149 × 5

London (1976) (4, repr. p. 10); Edinburgh 1976 (4, p. 14)

Konnertz pp 227, 229, 269 repr. pl. 412

imagery in this work and in the wooden reliefs of this
od can be related to several graphics, such as the suite for
les Rennie Mackintosh 1975 (D3.8-13).

Pikabio

ze, 1975

60 × 5 (edition of 3)

London 1976 (3, repr. p. 11) – (also repr. p. 1: the artist
wooden version of Pikabio in his Berlin studio at
ousser Damm, 1975).

For Victor Hugo

ze, s. 'E. Paolozzi', 1975

15 × 12

London 1976 (5, repr. p. 9)

general form of this work may be compared to the
mmage à Bruckner project of 1977 (D1.2).

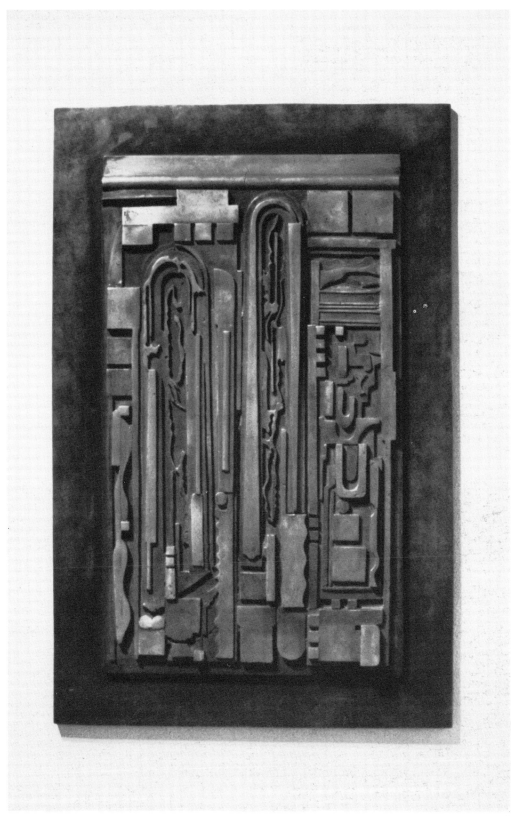

B1.12

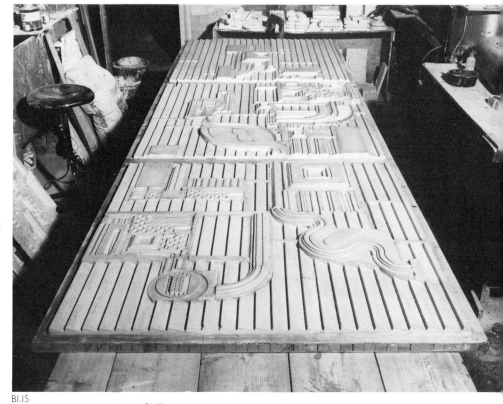

Bl.14-17 **Reliefs for the doors of the Hunterian Gallery, Glasgow University**
Plaster, 1976
99 x 103

Bl.15

Bl.16

Bl.17

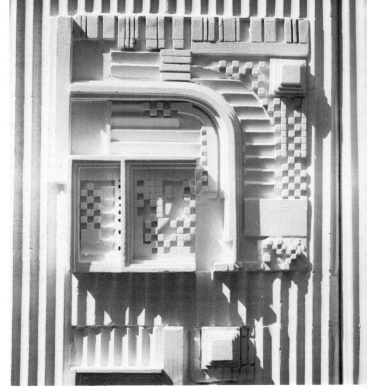

8 Study for Hamburg Wall Relief

od, 1978

x 54 x 5.3

Cologne 1979 repr.p. 52 (also repr. of Paolozzi working
full-scale plaster model, p. 51) ; London 1984 p. 24 (repr.
elief in situ.)

finished work consists of 6 bronze reliefs installed in pairs
h pair 172 x 80.5 cms) framed by original surrounds.
y were a private commission but are on full view to the
ic in their siting on an exterior wall of an apartment
ling at Moorweidenstrasse 3, Hamburg.

9 Study for Hamburg Wall Relief

n, 1978

5 x 54 x 5.3

0 Small Landscape I

er, 1979

x 22.5 x 2.5

es to **Camera** (DI.6) and **Matamalla** (DI.3-5).

1 Study for Monchengladbach Wall Relief

er and plywood, painted, 1979

x 35.5 x 3

London 1984 pp. 22, 23 (repr. of relief in situ p. 22)
mmissioned by the City of Monchengladbach for their new
fication centre. The finished relief is formed from 3-
ensional strips of stainless steel which stand out from the
incorporating cast shadows into the work.

2 Rhino

od, 1980

31.5 x 4.5

London 1981

work together with the larger **PIANO for LN and STA**
shown at the Tate Gallery's 1981 'Sculpture for the Blind'
bition. Both are intended to be explored by touch rather
sight, and comprise intricate relief surfaces and moving
ents. Whilst **Piano** is based on the height and reach of the
, the smaller dimensions of Rhino corresponds to the
ed reach of a child. They are both 'assemblages' of found-
cts: parts of a piano, discarded materials from the Royal
ege of Art and pieces of children's wooden construction
from China.

23 PIANO for LN and STA

od, 1980

x 83 x 7

. London 1981

Konnertz 1984 pp. 256, 257 repr. pls. 461, 462
title refers to the artists Louise Nevelson and Sophie
eber-Arp, both of whom work in wood and relief
pture.

Plate III

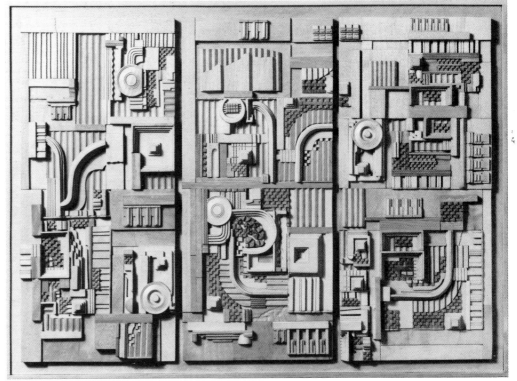

BI.18

BI.19

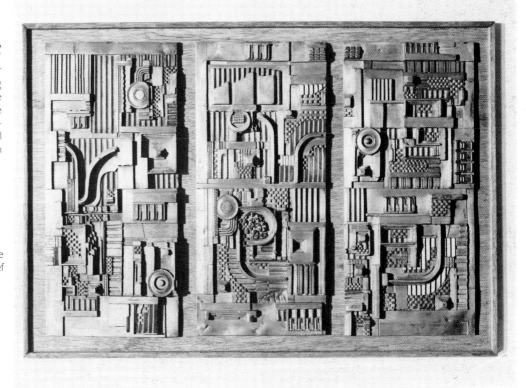

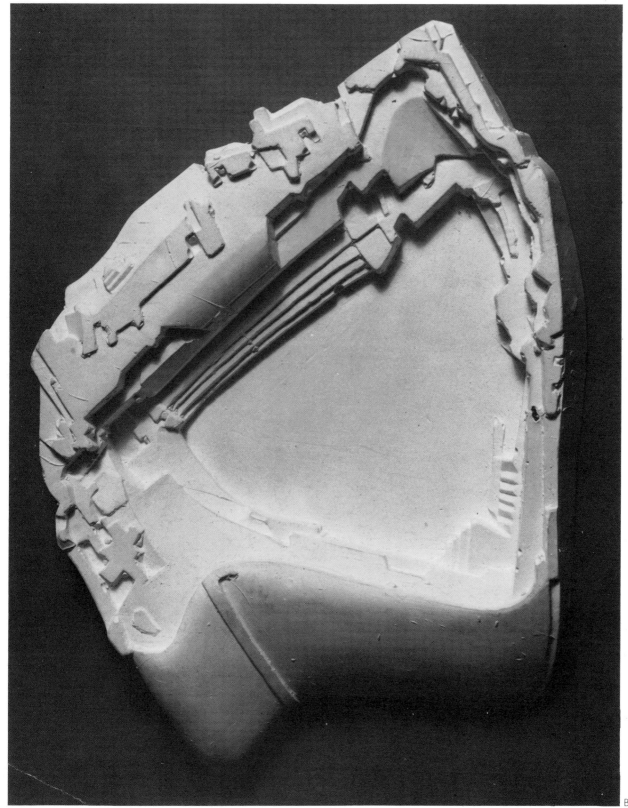

BI.20
FROM CLEISH TO CLO

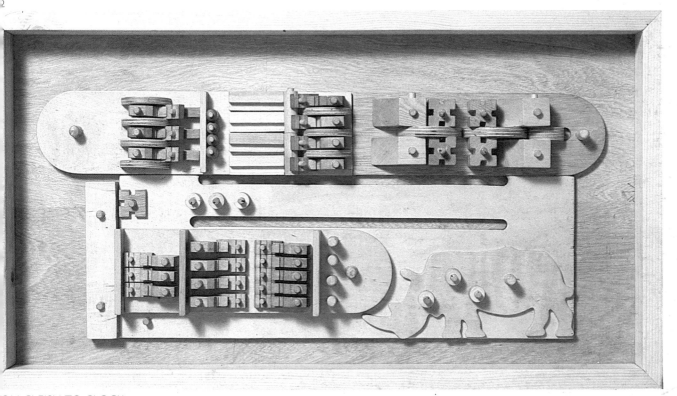

24 **Clock**
...ined wood and resin, 1983
...5 × 5
...h. London 1984
... Konnertz 1984 pp. 257, 269, repr. pl. 471
...related circular design in xerox is illustrated in Konnertz,
...84 pl. 270.
...me of the motifs in the relief first appeared in the
...eenprint **Ciao Picasso** (B3.9).

...1 **Southern Siphnian Frieze**
...ollage, sd '1946 Eduardo Paolozzi'
...5 × 24.5

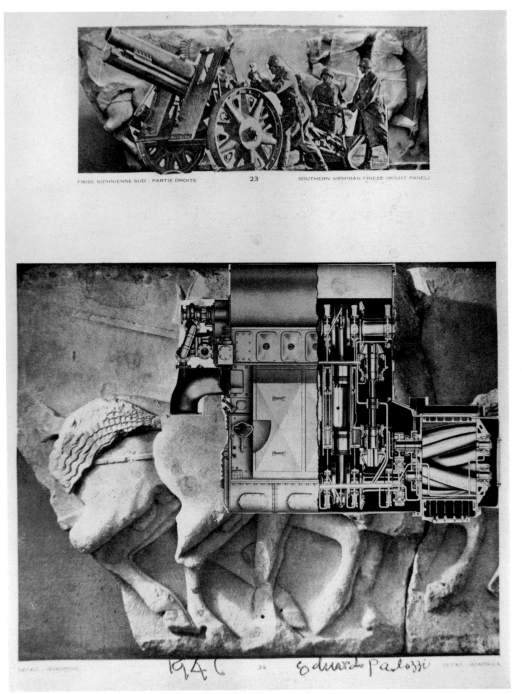

FRISE SIPHNIENNE SUD : PARTIE DROITE   23   SOUTHERN SIPHNIAN FRIEZE (RIGHT PANEL)

B2.1

B2.2

B2.2 **Cathédrale de la Ste Trinité**
Collage, sd 'E Paolozzi 1946'
25 x 32.75

B2.3 **Cage Work of Wood**
Collage, sd 'E Paolozzi 1946'
19.75 x 13.5

B2.4 **Port Maritime**
Collage, sd 'E Paolozzi 1946'
25.5 x 32.75

B2.4

B2.3

FROM CLEISH TO CLOC

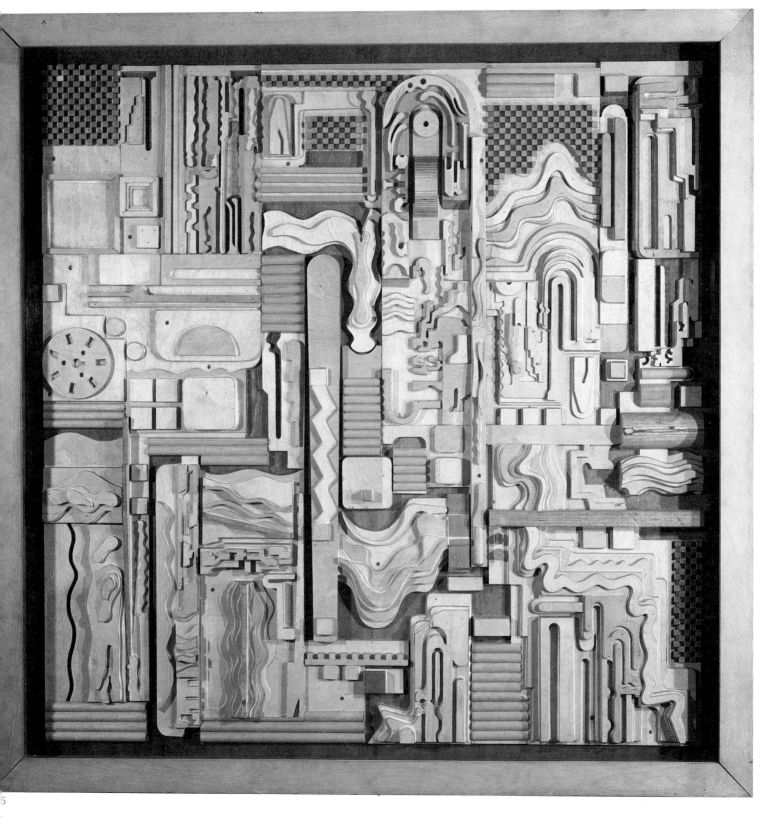

Bl.9

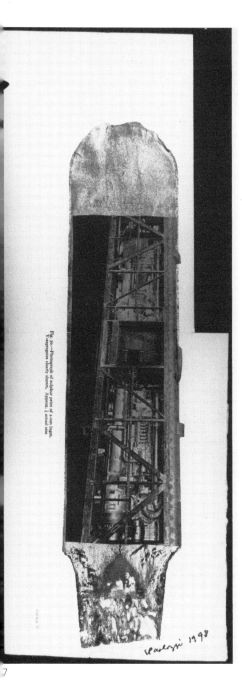

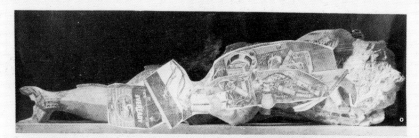

Above: 3. Herakles wrestling with Triton.   Below: 4. Three-bodied monster.
Pedimental groups in high relief from the earlier Hekatompedon (*poros* stone).
Athens, Acropolis Museum. (P. 19).

B2.5

Vista del Santuari i la muntanya.
Vista del Santuario y la montaña.   Ansicht des Gnadenortes und des Berges.
Vue du Sanctuaire et de la montagne.
Veduta del Santuario e della montagna.   A view of the Sanctuary and the mountain.

7

5 Pedimental Groups in High Relief
llage, sd 'E Paolozzi 1946'
5 × 23.75

6 Vista del Sanctuari
llage inscr. 'London E Paolozzi 1946-7 Cartwright Gdns'
25 × 26.25

7 Two Ton Ingot
llage, sd 'E Paolozzi 1948'
5 × 12.25   B2.6

OM CLEISH TO CLOCK

B2.8 Untitled
Pencil, sd 'E Paolozzi 1972'
24.5 × 34
Nos. B2.8-11 all relate to the Cleish Ceiling design. A number
of them, and other related drawings, have been exhibited at
Hannover 1974-5, Berlin 1975, London 1976, Edinburgh
1976, A.C.G.B. 1976-7, and Kassel 1978. Reproductions can
be found in some of the exhibition catalogues and in Konnertz,
1984, pls. 278, 379, 382.

B2.9 Untitled
Pencil, sd 'E.Paolozzi 1973'
26.5 × 36

B2.10 Untitled
Pencil, crayon, ink, sd 'Eduardo Paolozzi 1974'
30.5 × 23
Exh. London 1976 (38), Edinburgh 1976 (31)

B2.11 Untitled
Pencil, sd 'E.Paolozzi 1974'
21 × 25.5

B2.9

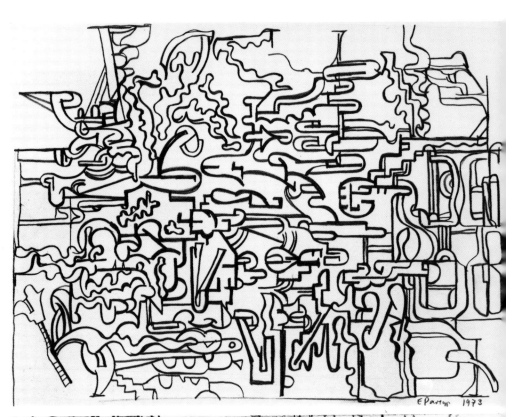

B2.11

FROM CLEISH TO CLO

B2.10

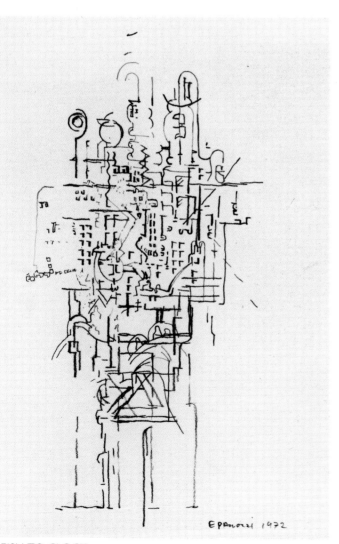

B3.1 War Games Revised from **Universal Electronic Vacuum**
Screenprint, 1967
101.5 × 68.6/91 × 61
Exh. Berkeley 1968 (repr. on cover)
Lit. Schneede 1970, Kirkpatrick 1970 pp. 99, 101, 102, 106, 107, 131-2 (repr. 80) London 1977, p. 27, Konnertz 1984 pp. 175ff, 203
See Plate XII

B3.2 Mr Peanut
Screenprint, 1970
80.5 × 55.5/ 69.5 × 48.5
Edition of 150 and 25 artists's proofs
The ground colour of each sheet printed in a different colour
Lit: London 1977, p. 43 (55)
See Plate XII
The design of this work is based upon a reproduction of a German abstract painting, interpreting organ music, which Paolozzi found in a 1927 edition of the magazine Kosmos. (See Konnertz, 1984, pp. 200-202). Paolozzi adapts this imagery in several other works of the 1970s; it is again closely followed in the screenprint **Leonardo** (B3.3), **Kosmos** (B3.4) and **Maahantai** (B3.5).

B3.3 Leonardo
Seenprint, 1974
64.5 × 50/60 × 42.2
Edition of 96 – of these a few proofs drawn on paper first given beige ground
Lit: London 1977 pp.44-45 (repr. pl. 23), Konnertz 1984 p. 202 (repr. pl. 374)

B3.4 Kosmos
Metal relief etching, 1975
65 × 50/51 × 35.75
Edition of 70

B3.5 Maahantai
Photogravure, 1975
80 × 50/62.5 × 42.75
Edition of 100

B3.6 Untitled
Woodcut, 1975
65 × 47/57 × 23c

B3.7 Untitled
Woodcut, 1975
65 × 47/60 × 27
A/P

B3.8 Appel-Calder
Screenprint, 1975
Edition of 500, 88 in different colourways, 100 × 70/75.5 54.5 Lit: London 1977 (188), Konnertz 1984 pp. 234, 26 repr. pl. 419

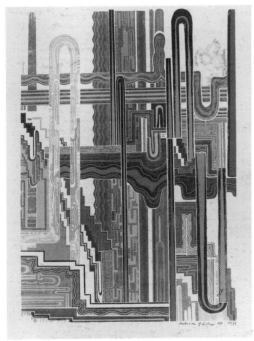

B3.3

B3.5

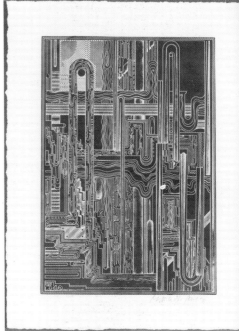

B3.4

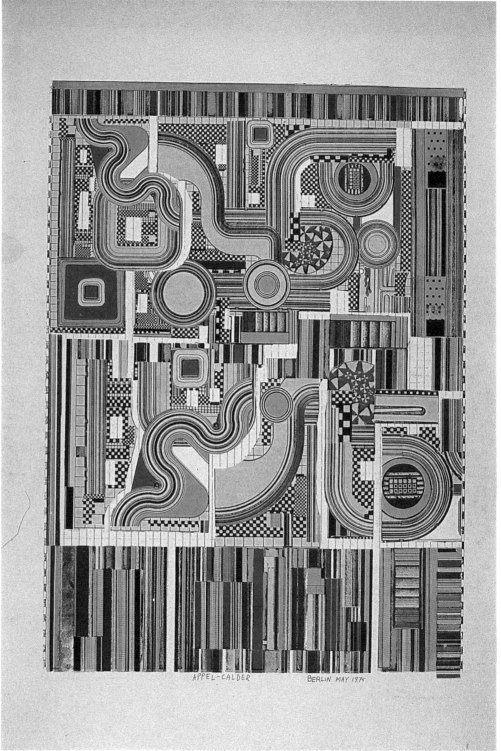

B3.8

B3.9 **Ciao Picasso**
Screenprint, 1975
Edition of 30, each sheet with individual colourways about 10
artist's proofs, 100 × 70/74.8 × 53cm
Some of the motifs in this print reappear in the circular relief
Clock (B1.24).

B3.10 **Untitled**
Woodcut, 1976
32.75 × 25/9 × 6cm

B3.11 **Untitled**
Woodcut, 1976
32.5 × 25cm/14.75 × 9.5cm

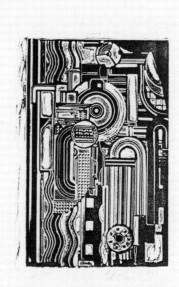

B3.10

B3.11

2 **Italian Landscape after Montaigne**
ning, 1984
× 51/31.75 × 49cm
on of 5

3 **Italian Landscape II**
ning, 1984
× 51/37.25 × 49.75cm

B3.12

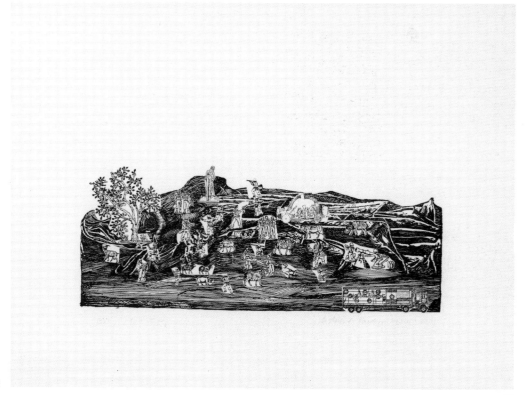

B3.13

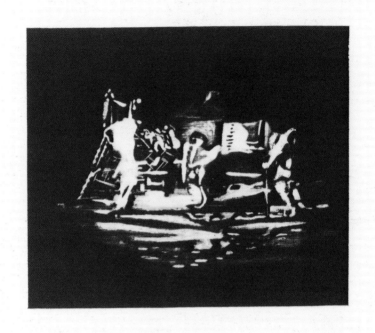

B3.14 **On the Moon**
Etching, 1984
67.5 × 51/23.75 × 28.5

HEROES AND DEITIES

Heroes and Deities

Key phrases, like key sculpture, take time to make. The arrival at a plastic iconography is just as difficult as a language. A few sculptures per year can alter other plastic values. **Eduardo Paolozzi 'Notes from a Lecture at the Institute of Contemporary Arts', Uppercase, No.I, 1958.**

In the 1950s Paolozzi created a new race of heroes and deities which looked entirely different from the biomorphic forms of Henry Moore. Mythological, religious and secular imagery was placed at the service of a modern sensibility, by the use of junkyard materials originally intended for other purposes. In 1958 Paolozzi called this a 'metamorphosis of rubbish', in 1963 'the comedy of waste'.[1] Twenty years on, the use of discarded materials is basically the same, although they are put through a different process to make relief sculpture.

The art brut and wilful distortions in Dubuffet's paintings, children's drawings and the art of the mentally disturbed, combined with the rough surfaces of ready-made machine components, provided an entirely new direction for Paolozzi's sculpture. The means of making these works is recognised as being associated with the ready-made principles of Dada and Surrealism, encountered in Paris in 1947, and the collage method with Raymond Roussel's 'Comment j'ai écrit certains de mes livres' which Paolozzi came across at about the same time. His intention was not to add to the repertoire of ephemeral ready-mades, which he regarded as mere mementoes or by-products, but to create sculpture of permanence and presence by using the methods of transformation and metamorphosis pioneered by the Surrealists thirty years before.[2]

In content and form some of these works resemble the sculpture of Giacometti, whom Paolozzi has recently acknowledged as being unquestionably the most impressive single artist he encountered in Paris. Having abandoned the Surrealist objects of the 1930s, Giacometti was then making his series of male figure studies. Attenuated and diminutive, some no bigger than a matchstick, they isolated Giacometti from his fellow artists of the previous decade, but in 1947 Giacometti showed Paolozzi what could be achieved by an obsessive spirit working alone with the simplest of materials: clay and a penknife.[3] Sartre recognised in Giacometti's sculpture an existentialist concern for man's condition; Paolozzi's gods and heroes stride across cultural barriers, their existence and the identity of their maker being in the found objects holding them together, or in their titles. **His Majesty the Wheel** (Cl. 6) refers not just to ideas of kingship in general and to the wheel

as a technological symbol, but specifically to current corruption by a Unit[ed] States trades union leader. **St Sebastian** (Cl. 4), martyr and Renaissan[ce] hero, is made into an icon-victim of contemporary man. One of the mo[st] celebrated images in paint of St Sebastian's martyrdom is by Pollaiuolo, w[ho] also made sculpture. That Paolozzi went on to make three further images [of] St Sebastian is of no small interest, for in his art the two media of painting a[nd] sculpture have been held in constant creative tension.

Paolozzi is now working on new figure studies (Cl. 20). The still-life [is] another recurring theme, and he intends to return to it, probably in drawin[gs] and prints in which his own work will appear. The still-life first made [its] appearance in a series of table sculptures of the late 1940s. It reappear[s] with a more mechanised edge in the **Mechanik's Bench** of 1963 (Cl. 12) and again ten years later, with found objects, in bronze (Cl. 18).

In 1962 Paolozzi temporarily abandoned the lost wax method for bron[ze] casting, and began to work at a small engineering factory in Ipswich. H[e] designed a series of patterns for elements prefabricated in aluminium wh[ich] could be grouped in different combinations to make sculpture. Th[e] geometry and smooth surfaces are in strong contrast to previous work, a[nd] to the sculpture he is making now. Whereas the bronzes of the 1950s ha[d] strong figurative character, the aluminium sculptures of the 1960s are mo[re] machine-like and less obviously anthropomorphic.

The double, or twin towers, were among the first sculptures to be ma[de] using the new method. To build the towers, models were first cut out [of] plywood, sent to pattern making shops for refining, and then cast [in] aluminium, bronze or gun metal. They were less 'studio orientated' th[an] before, and preserved the anonymity of the machine-shop floor prior [to] their assembly. Paolozzi has said that the twin towers were linked in his mi[nd] to the machine concept behind the photolithograph **Inkwells** of 196[ ] which uses the image of a locomotive. Their strong architectural associati[on] was evoked by seeing German municipal buildings (Paolozzi had been livi[ng] in Hamburg in 1962); and the radiating circular fans which bridge the towe[rs] came from pastry slicers traditionally used by German housewives.

'A recent book on Rodin mentions the way the great sculptor h[ad] transitions of the portraits cast so that a spontaneous stage could be fus[ed] and held in reserve for future development. One photograph shows t[he] large collection of legs, feet and heads made by Rodin to enable him [to] fabricate figures outside the limits of preconception. Plastic metapho[r] generated by the inner cinema of mind, a cameraless photography of t[he] inner soul. The Rathaus in Zurich dwarfed by a frog represents not o[nly] poetic ambiguity but a personal hypothesis.'

Paolozzi has become increasingly interested in Rodin's process of casti[ng,] recasting, and modifying his plasters as a staging post in the development [of] the sculptured image.[6] Over the years he has followed with interest t[he] revaluation of such practices by Rodin, and the aesthetic as well [as] philosophic implications which Rodin's reproductive methods have [for] making sculpture and graphic art. In contrast to the architectural towe[rs] with their feet firmly planted on the earth, a quite different effect is made [by] those sculptures with curvilinear and tubular components. **Rio** (not in t[he] exhibition), a large bronze sculpture of 1964-5, in six parts, has a dispositi[on] analogous to Rodin's **Burghers of Calais**. Instead of stability, works such [as] **Poem for the Trio MRT**, (Cl.13) **Girot** (Cl.14) and **Gexhi** (Cl.1[ ]

...rest movement. Their formal language, which is shared by **As is When** (..2-14), can be traced to the Laocoön which for more than twenty years ...been a rich source of inspiration, and from time to time is quoted in ...ings and screen prints (D3.18-24).

...n May of this year Paolozzi made a new plaster cast after a bronze table ...ion of the Laocoon he had once owned. He then dismembered the ...ter, and is now recasting its parts in order to introduce into new ...tionships with sculpture component heads and limbs from other ...rces, which in their turn have undergone similar transformations, ...ections and recasting. Wheras Paolozzi is at present making moulds, ...ring plaster and altering casts, the comparative physical intransigence of ...al sculpture required a different set of creative responses. Most of the ...pture of around 1964-5 is resolutely three dimensional, but because ...lozzi was also then making the collages for **As is When**, the question ...e of the relationship between painting and sculpture, as it did for other ...sh artists such as Anthony Caro. Paolozzi's answer was to paint his ...pture with the same range of colours he had used to screen his prints. ...original reason for painting **Hamlet**' he has said, 'was to relate it to my ...ges'.[7] **Hamlet in a Japanese Manner** (Cl. 15) was painted twice, in ...6 and 1971. Both colour schemes relate to the subjects and designs of his ...enprints from those years; but the sculpture was finally stripped down to ...metal before being acquired by the Glasgow Museum. In 1965 Paolozzi ...cribed his interest in the relationship between painting and sculpture to ...ard Hamilton.

...'Well, I think one might perhaps be able to reach an ultimate, which is the ...ving together even closer of painting and sculpture by actually painting ...sculpture itself. There is another possibility, with a silk screen, which is ...ething I am involved with and have been for a long time. After the screen ...ade up, certain geometrical ingredients, such as variations on the square ...he curve, the stripe, the circle, could be applied by the transfer process to ...geometric solids of the sculpture, so that you have geometry on two ...ls. This I think would be an ultimate of a kind. I think that modern ...pture of the best kind has been in and out of the idea of the painted ...pture, approaching the point where you can't distinguish between ...ting and sculpture, where they cross over in an original way. This would ...a goal for me.'[8]

...While the sombre subject-matter of **Cloud Atomic Laboratory** ...18-25) has already been noted, the silver whites and ink blacks of these ...ts, with those from the companion series **Conditional Probablity** ...hine, probably made no small contribution in preparing for a return to ...ing relief sculpture, in which monochrome shading is an integral part of ...visual experience. When Paolozzi started making reliefs in the early ...0s the colours in his prints began to change, from brilliant primaries to ...pastel shades, a process that culminates in the **Calcium Light Night** ...es of 1974-76 (C3. 26-34). In subsequent woodcuts and etchings ...C3. 39) the primary optical effect lies with the relationship of the inked ...ge to white paper, while the extreme formal purity of working with ...ter has resulted in several relief prints, white on white, which carry no ink ...l. Significantly, colour is again making an appearance in his most recent ...pture, in the **Clock** relief, and in heads such as **Electric Bishop** ...produced on the cover).

Notes

1. 'Metamorphosis of Rubbish – Mr Paolozzi Explains his Process', **The Times**, 2 May 1958; 'Notes by the Sculptor' in Lawrence Alloway, **Metallization of a Dream**, London, 1963.

2. Eduardo Roditi, **Dialogues on Art**, London, 1960 (revised ed. Santa Barbara, 1980), pp. 157-68.

3. Eduardo Paolozzi, BBC, Radio 3, March 1984.

4. Eduardo Paolozzi, 'Where Reality Lies', **The Oxford Art Journal**, Vol. 6, No. 1, 1983, pp. 39-40.

5. Eduardo Paolozzi, 'Collage or a Scenario for a Comedy of Critical Hallucination' in **Eduardo Paolozzi, Collages and Drawings**, Anthony d'Offay 1977 (exh. cat.).

6. See Albert Elsen, **Rodin Rediscovered**, Washington, 1981 (exh. cat.), especially Chapter V 'When the Sculptures Were White'.

7. Bernhard Kerbert, 'Skulptur und Farbe', **Kunstforum**, 60 April 1983, p. 69.

8. Richard Hamilton, 'Interview with Eduardo Paolozzi', **Arts Yearbook**, 8, 1965. (Reprinted in **Eduardo Paolozzi, Sculpture, Drawings, Collages and Graphics**, Arts Council Exhibition, 1976-77, p. 37.)

C1.1 **Robot**

Bronze, edition of six, 1956
48.5 × 22 × 15
Exh: London 1958 (24) repr; British Pavilion. XXX Biennale
International 1960; Hannover 1974-5 (10); Berlin 1975 (18);
Lit: Konnertz 1984 p. 87 (repr. pl. 167)
Created with a similar found-object technique as that used in
his 'machine' head sculptures of the 1950s (for example
A1.7), the integration of the human figure and the machine is
also explored through Paolozzi's interest in science-fiction, in
which the robot as an iconographical figure has been a staple
element. See Plate XVI

C1.2 **Small Monument**

Bronze, 1956
33 cm high
Private collection
Lit: Middleton 1963 (repr.) Exh: N.Y. 1958.

C1.3 **Cyclops**

Bronze, 1957
101 × 30.5 × 20.3
The Tate Gallery
Exh: New York 1960 (3: repr. on cover); London 1968 (10:
repr. on cover); Hannover 1974-5 (11: repr. p. 74); Berlin
1975 (20: repr. p. 82);
Lit: Roditi 1980 (repr. p. 156) Konnertz 1984 (repr.
pl. 181)
A bronze head of the same title was also exhibited at the
Hanover Gallery, London in 1958 (6).

C1.4 **St Sebastian I**

Bronze, 1957
217 × 86 × 41
Private Collection
Exh: New York 1958 repr.; Hannover 1974-5 (12) p. 75;
Berlin 1975 (21: repr. p. 83)
Lit: Schneede 1970 pp. 12, 13 repr. pl. 29; Kirkpatrick 1970
p. 30; Konnertz 1984 pp. 87, 91,95 repr.pl. 179
St. Sebastian No.II, 1957, is in the Solomon R. Guggenheim
Museum, New York. **St Sebastian III**, 1958-9 is in the
Rijksmuseum, Amsterdam and another sculpture of the same
title is in a private collection. 'My occupation can be described
as the ERECTION OF HOLLOW GODS with the head like
an eye, the centre part like a retina. This figure in three parts
can be described in the use of a form of principle of
Architectural Anatomy. A base contains the title, date and
author in landscape letters, the legs as decorated columns/or
towers. The torso like a tornado-struck town, a hillside or the
slums of Calcutta. A bronze framework containing symbols
resembling bent mechanism. An automata totally exposed,
with ciphers. A statement printed on the back. (Paolozzi, from
'Notes from a lecture at the Institute of Contemporary Arts
1958' reproduced in Kirkpatrick, 1970, p. 130).

C1.5 **Standing Figure**

Bronze, 1958
32 × 11 × 9
Exh: Hannover 1974-5 (15: repr. p. 72); Berlin 1975 (25:
repr. p. 80)

C1.4

His Majesty the Wheel
…e, 1958-9
…m high
…e Collection
…iddleton 1963 repr.; Scheede 1970 pp. 12,14 repr.
…2,33; Kirkpatrick 1970 pp. 43,44 repr. pl. 31; Konnertz
…p. 116 repr. pls. 187, 188
…heel, which Paolozzi regarded as 'a quickly read symbol
…man-made object', recurs as a motif in numerous works.
…tle of this sculpture has several layers of meaning; it
…s in part from a Time magazine story about an American
…union leader, Jimmy Hoffa, and by association refers to
…al corruption and the slang terminology of 'big wheel' or
…(See Kirkpatrick, 1970)

CI.7 **Tyrannical Tower**
Bronze, 1961
183 × 60.5 38
Private collection
Exh: NY 1962 (11: repr. on cover); Hannover 1974-5 (16) repr .p. 89; Berlin 1975 (27) repr. p. 97;
Lit: Middleton 1963 repr; Schneede 1970 p. 14 repr. pl. 36; Kirkpatrick 1970 pp. 47, 49, 55 repr. pl. 36; Konnertz 1984 pp. 116, 120 repr. pl. 231
This work is transitional between the tower figures such as **His Majesty the Wheel** (CI.6) and the machine-style towers such as **Imperial War Museum** (CI.10). Unlike the later works which utilize regular machined forms, the elements of this sculpture were hand-made in a wax-to-bronze technique.

CI.8 **Bishop of Kuban**
Painted aluminium, 1962
208 × 90 × 60
Private collection
Exh: London 1971 (44); Hannover 1974-5 (17: repr.p. 91); Berlin 1975 (29: repr. p. 99)
Lit: Schneede 1970 pp. 16, 19 repr. p. 48 in unpainted state; Konnertz 1984 pp. 120, 122, 128 repr. pl. 246 in painted state

CI.9 **Twin Towers of the Sfinx-State I**
Bronze, 1962
Whitworth Art Gallery, University of Manchester

CI.7

CI.8

Imperial War Museum

nium, 1962

136 x 51

Newcastle upon Tyne 1965 (3); Hanover Gallery
on? 1968 repr.; London 1971 (41: repr.70); Berlin 1975
repr.p. 102

eichardt 1963 p. 86 repr.pl. 7 (as 'Twin Towers of the
State Double Reflected'); Schneede 1970 p. 14 repr.
Paolozzi 1983 pp. 39-40 repr. fig. 2; Konnertz 1984
3, repr. pl. 249

was one of the first sculptures Paolozzi made at the
h Engineering works of C.W. Juby after his return to
nd in the early 1960s. Like other sculpture of this period it
ins ready-made elements brought back from Germany.
e works, according to Paolozzi '... are a kind of
nentary on Germany – for example, they remind me of
an town halls, and the circular disk comes from a cutter
erman housewife still uses to cut equal slices of cake.'
ozzi, in the Oxford Art Journal 1983 p. 40). The
tion in the catalogue of the London 1972 Exhibition
above) shows the sculpture in a different state with only
ead of 6 finials and a different arrangement of the central
n. This is similar to the 'Twin Towers of the Sfinx State
ole Reflected' illustrated in Reichardt 1963 pl. 7.

Wittgenstein at Casino

ed aluminium, 1963

139 x 49.5

City Art Galleries

Hannover 1974-5 (19); Berlin 1975 (34: repr. p. 104
ted, as 'Wittgenstein at Casino I'); A.C.G.B. 1976 (7:
p. 11 (painted) and p. 46 (painted)

eichardt 1964 pp. 155-6; Schneede 1970 pp. 14, 19 repr.
(unpainted); Konnertz 1984 pp. 128, 130, 163 repr.
55 (painted)

genstein is the subject of the set of screenprints **As is**
n.

work in its painted state illustrates Paolozzi's interest in
ining media. 'I think that modern sculpture of the best
has been in and out of the idea of the painted sculpture,
paching the point where you can't distinguish between
ng and sculpture, where they cross over in an original
This would be a goal for me.' (Paolozzi in an interview
Richard Hamilton in 1965, reproduced in A.C.G.B. 1976-
alogue p. 37).
Plate XVII

CI.9

CI.13

CI.16

CI.14

Mechanik's Bench

...inium, 1963
... × 182.5 × 56
...Tate Gallery
... Berlin 1964-5 'New Realisten and Pop Art' (78: repr. f.
... London 1971 (46: repr. pl. 73); Berlin 1975 (36: repr.
...)
...irkpatrick 1970 p. 62 repr. pl. 49; Schneede 1970 p. 19
... pl. 50; Konnertz 1984 pp. 130,131 repr. pl. 260
...work was partly inspired by a series of old-fashioned
...ings of mechanical still-lifes, and the component elements
...aolozzi's own machine sculpture lying about waiting
...bly. 'Combination of furniture and machine / Hybrid /
...ination on a table . . . / A cycle of changing references
...r together / A collection of human artifaces / Switch gear
...man hand factors assembled, edited, rearranged / New
...gies cross referenced and cross detailed . . . /
...ANIKS BENCH.' Paolozzi in 'Metafisikal Translation'
... Paolozzi took up the subject of the table and still life again
...74 with **Bronze Table** I and II (Cl.18 and 19).

Cl.13 Poem for the Trio MRT
Aluminium, 1964
216 × 218 × 111.8
Leeds City Art Galleries
Exh: London 1971 (48); Hannover 1974-75 (29: repr.
p. 121); Berlin 1975 (37: repr. pp. 121); ACGB 1976 (8: repr.
pp. 12, 47)
Lit: Schneede 1970, p. 20, repr. pl. 57; Konnertz 1984,
pp. 130, 134, 166 repr. pl. 273
The form of the sculpture is close to the imagery of the **As is
When** screenprints (C3.2-14) which immediately followed. It
combines something of the myth of the Trojan priest and his
two sons strangled by the serpent, as depicted by the sculptor
of the Laocoon with the three artist heroes of the Russian
Constructivist movement referred to in the title – Malevich,
Rodchenko and Tatlin.

Cl.14 Girot
Aluminium, 1964
212 × 218 × 112

Exh: Newcastle upon Tyne 1965 (13); Stuttgart 1969 (13);
Middelheim, Antwerp 1969 (82) repr; London 1971 (49:
repr. p. 72); Berlin 1975 (39: repr. p. 106)
Lit: Konnertz 1984 pp. 134, 166 repr. 271
There is also a screenprint with the same title.

Cl.15 Hamlet in a Japanese Manner
Aluminium: 3 elements, 1966
109 × 110 × 97, 154 × 185 × 185, 165 × 175 × 110
Glasgow Art Gallery and Museum
Exh: London 1966 'Sculpture in the Open Air' (33) repr.;
London 1971 (50); Berlin 1975 (42: repr. p. 111, in first
painted state)
Lit: Konnertz 1984 pp. 136, 138, 142, 147,148,151,257 repr.
pls. 278, 279 (in second painted and also third state 1976).
This work has been painted in several different colour
schemes, but was stripped down by the artist in 1981. For
Paolozzi's view on painting sculpture in 1965 see **Wittgen-
stein at Casino**. About the genesis of **Hamlet . . .**, Paolozzi
has commented, 'At that time in London there was a very

Cl.15

modern and exciting production of Hamlet by an Italian theatre group who turned most conventional concepts of the play upside down. There was other theatre imported from Japan which gave me the idea of mixing cultures – not a new idea but at the very least one which has fertilised Western art for almost a century. Almost like self-fulfilling prophecy, I was able to actually work in Japan three years later at an engineering firm creating a sculpture for Expo '70'. (See D1.1) Paolozzi, quoted in Kunstforum International no. 60, April 1983, p. 69ff.

C1.16 Gexhi
Polished steel, 1967
182 × 375 × 171
Aberdeen Art Gallery and Museum
Exh. London, Hannover Gallery ? 1968 repr.; Stuttgart 1969 (17)
Lit: Kirkpatrick 1970 p. 73 repr. pl. 62

C1.17 Between the Acts
Chromed steel, 1967
160 × 65 × 89
Private collection

C1.18 Bronze Table (Still Life)
Bronze, 1974-5
131 × 87.5 × 64
Exh: Basle Art Fair, British Pavilion 1975 repr.; London 1976 (30) Edinburgh 1976 (18) – a related drawing **Study for Table Sculpture 1974** was exhibited in Edinburgh in 1976 (6: repr. p. 22).

C1.18

9 **Bronze Table II**
nze, 1974
x 89 × 66
: Berlin 1975 (71: repr. pl. 31); London 1976 (27: repr.
9)

C1.20 **Torso**
Bronze, 1984
20 × 22 × 8.5 on 3cm wood base

9

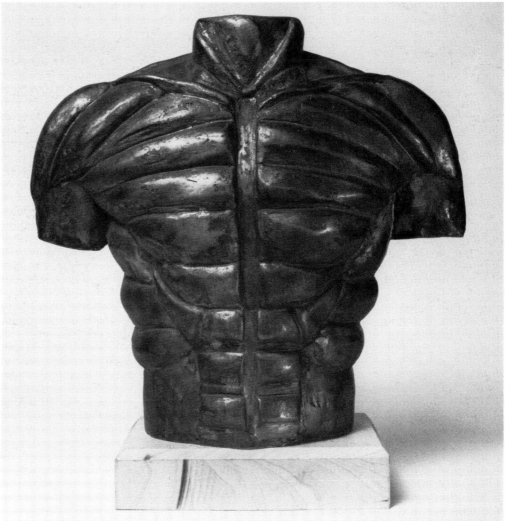

C1.20

C2.1 Nike des Paionios
Collage, sd 'E Paolozzi 1946'
25.75 x 18.25/19.9 x 10.6
Lit: Konnertz 1984 p. 31 repr. pl. 48

C2.2 Welsh War Memorial
Collage, sd 'E Paolozzi 1946'
19.75 x 13.5

C2.3 What is the Sun?
Collage, sd 'E Paolozzi 1946'
40.5 x 27.5

C2.4 Sadistic Confession
Collage, sd 'E Paolozzi 1946-7'
33 x 25.5

C2.5 Your Physique
Collage
33.75 x 23.75
Private Collection
Lit: Konnertz 1984 repr. pl. 362

C2.6 Putting on the Clay
Collage, sd 'E Paolozzi 1947'
19.5 x 14
Lit: Konnertz 1984 repr. pl. 50
Part of the image relates to **Cagework of Wood** (B2.3)
is derived from an illustration in 'Modelling and Sculpture
Albert Toft

C2.1

C2.2

C2.6

HOLIDAY

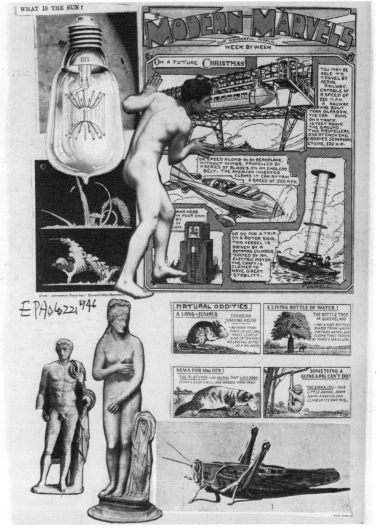

C2.3

C2.8 **Cory Coffee**
Collage, sd 'E Paolozzi 1948'
38 x 25
See Plate XX

C2.9 **Drink Dr Pepper**
Collage, sd 'E Paolozzi 1948'
35.75 x 23.75

C2.10 **Composizione Par Parere**
Collage, ins. 'Summer Paris Eduardo Paolozzi 1948'
35.75 x 23.75

C2.11 **Colloquio**
Collage, sd 'E Paolozzi 1949'
38 x 28.5

C2.12 **Heart's Delight**
Collage, sd 'E Paolozzi 1949'
39 x 26

C2.13 **Alive with Innovations**
Collage, sd 'E Paolozzi 1949'
24.5 x 37.5
See Plate XX

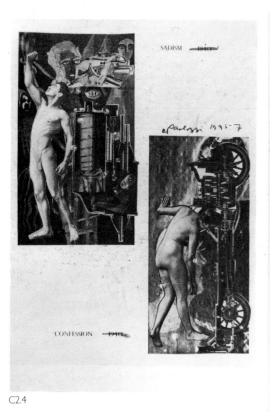

C2.4

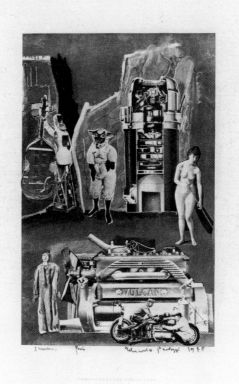

C2.10

C2.11

HEROES AND DEI

C2.12

C2.9

C2.13

C2.8

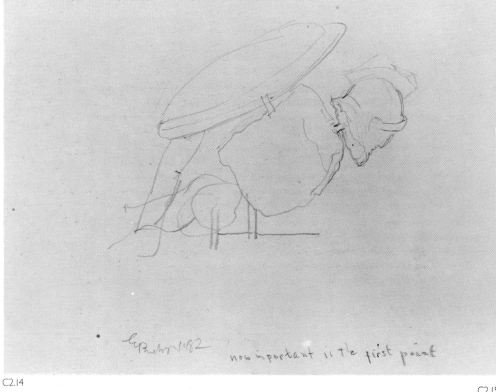

C2.14

16

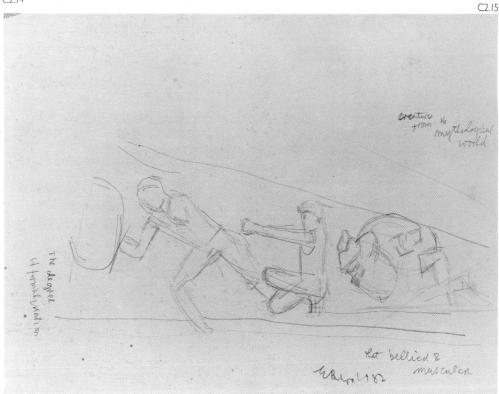

C2.15

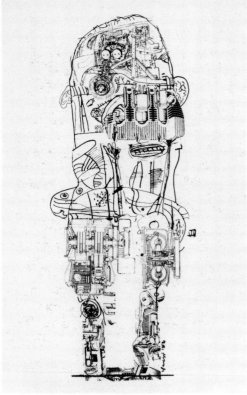

C3.1

C3.2

C3.3

Standing Figure

nprint (1962), 1956-8

x 37

n of 10

chneede 1970 repr. pl. 16 London 1977 p. 18 (7),
ertz 1984, pl. 58, repr. pl. 176

-14 **As is When**

reenprints, poster and text, 1965

66/ 83 × 55 (maximum)

n of 65 and 12 artist's proofs, each sheet printed with
dual colourway

oster

s is When: Artificial Sun
s is When: Tortured Life
s is When: Experience
s is When: Reality
s is When: Wittgenstein as Soldier
s is When: Wittgenstein in New York
s is When: Parrot
s is When: Futurism at Lenabo
is When: Assembling Reminders for a particular
se
s is When: The Spirit of the Snake
s is When: He must, so to speak, throw away the
er
s is When: Wittgenstein at the Cinema admires Betty
e

chneede 1970 p. 9 repr. p. 7; Kirkpatrick pp. 94ff, 106,
repr. pl. 72, 74, 75; London 1977 pp. 23-4; Konnertz
pp. 114, 134, 158, 159, 162ff, 175, 226, 261, 267. repr.
0, 311, 315, 317.

series of screenprints, described as the medium's first
erpiece, was developed from collages made in 1964 and
They relate to the life and work of the philosopher
enstein, each print incorporating quotations from his
gs or from the biographies by Norman Malcolm and
ge von Wright. There are three figurative biographical
and nine more abstract sheets, based on Wittgenstein's
sophy.
Plate XVIII)

C3.4

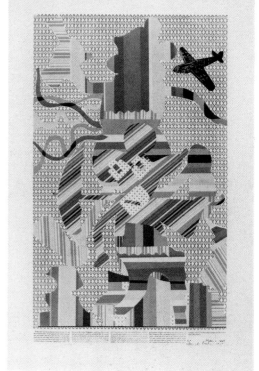

C3.14

C3.6

C3.7

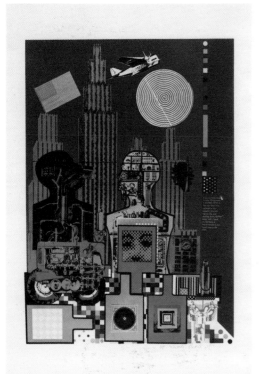

C3.8

C3.9

C3.10

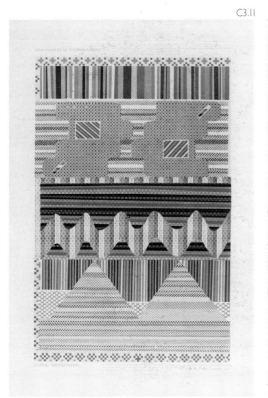

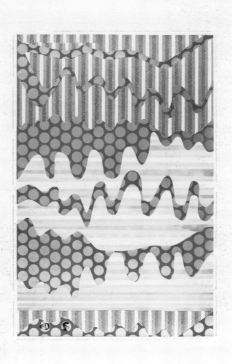

Fig.3

C3.15

5 Pig
ogravure, 1970
21
mage relates to the photogravure series **Cloud Atomic**
oratory (C3.18-25).

6 **20 Traumatic Twinges**
graph, 1970
25.4
the series **General Dynamic Fun**. Vol. 2 of **Moonstrips**
ire News. The image is of the robot heroine from Fritz
's film 'Metropolis', 1927.

7 **No Heroes Developed**
ograph, 1970
25.4
the series General Dynamic Fun.

C3.17

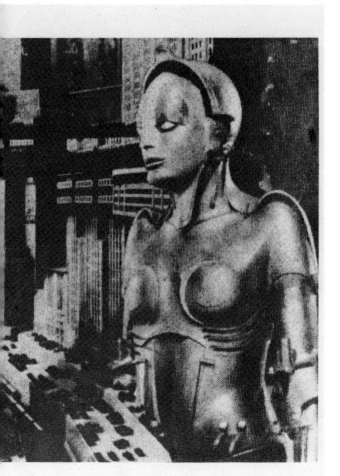

C3.16

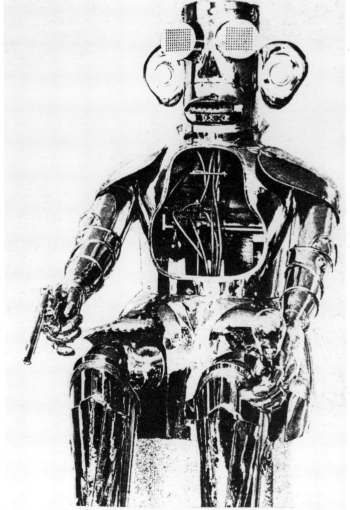

C3.19

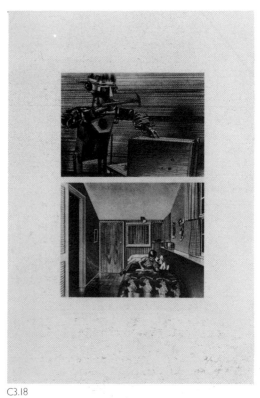

C3.18

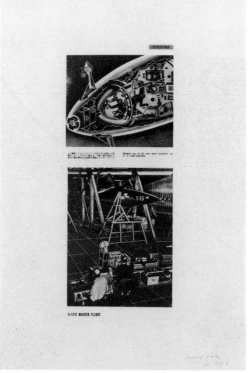

C3.21

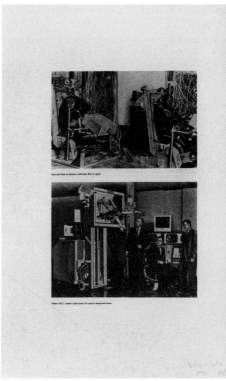

C3.23

C3.22

8-25 Cloud Atomic Laboratory (Science and Fantasy
e Technological World)
otogravures and text in tandem images, 1971
x 36 (sheet size: various plate sizes)
ductory text by Eduardo Paolozzi.
arco Robot Nailing a Wooden Box and Little Boy on his
n his Room
x 24
ull of Test Dummy and U.S.S.R Proton-Synchron
rophysical Laboratory
x 52.3
e Robot Robert Voulait Aller a New York Mais Le
iger Est Trop Lourd/TWA Plain-Steps-Caps 14 Persons
two Stewardesses and Wonder Toy
x 35.

21 Culture/Monkeys may be the Next Space Travellers on
U.S. made Satellites and X.15's Maiden Flight
38.3 × 18.6
22 Public Torso on Lorry on a Manhattan Street for Bond
Clothes for Men and Varga Billboard Girl
22 × 47.6
23 Chimpanzee in a Test Box Designed for Space Flight and
Mobot Mark I
34.7 × 24
24 Space Age Archaeology
Fathers and Sons
23.2 × 41.5
25 Television Series 'Lost in Space' Robot as in 'Forbidden
Planet' and Soviet Dog and Man Exit From Space
Chamber
26.5 × 37.7

Lit: London 1977 pp. 42-3 (88-95); Konnertz pp. 64, 101,
188, 192ff repr. pls. 355, 359, 360.
In a subtle blend of science reality and fiction, these images are
a distortion of the apparent photographic truth. Paolozzi
employed Lyndon Haywood, trained in commercial advertising techiques, to paint the images with an airbrush, creating
what Paolozzi has termed 'paintings based on photographs.' In
his introduction to the series Paolozzi wrote, 'a difficulty in
assessing the aesthetic value of these works is emphasised by
the monolithic concepts concerning all the great mechanical
arts. The schism that separates Space Age Engineering,
technical photography, film making and types of street art from
fine art activities is for many people/artists unbridgeable.
Within the grand system of paradoxes the same theme of this
portfolio is the Human Predicament. Content enlarged by
precision. History shaded into the grey scale as in the television
tube'.

C3.25

C3.26-34 **Calcium Light Night**

Series of 9 prints for Charles Ives
Screenprints, 1974-6
99 × 69
Edition of 200 and 25 artists's proofs
26 The Children's Hour
27 Largo to Presto
28 Central Park in the Dark Some 40 Years Ago
29 Allegro Moderato Fireman's Parade
30 Aeschylus and Socrates
31 From Early Italian Poets
32 Four German Songs
33 Calcium Night Light
34 Nettleton (See Plate XIX)
Lit: London 1977 pp. 48-9; St Andrews 1979; Paolozzi 1983 p. 43 repr. fig. 9; Konnertz 1984 pp. 215, 217ff, 225, 261, 267, repr. pls. 399, 401, 402, 403, 404.

Charles Ives (1874-1954), born in Connecticut and a contemporary of Schoenberg, worked in almost complete isolation but developed ideas comparable to those of avant-garde European composers. The titles of Paolozzi's suite are taken from, and are interpretations of, songs by Ives. 'Central Park in the Dark' has been derived by Ives from a news item about a runaway horse in Central Park and the overall title of the suite refers to a student's torchlight procession. Ives's unorthodox formal experiments and multi-layering of musical sources could be seen to parallel Paolozzi's methods of visual composition. Paolozzi has said of this series that he 'wanted to look at the idea of the relationship between collage and making images. With Chris Betambeau, who did the printing, I was able to use a variety of printing techniques in each print including adding colours photographically, handpainting some photographic areas on the screens, mechanical tints, under and over exposing photographically, hand-stippling and embossing. In the series between six and twelve screens were used for each print. The overall theme in addition to the dedication to Charles Ives is an attempt to find some visual comparison between music and drawing.' (Pao 1983).

In 1979 Paolozzi said of the last screenprint in the se 'Nettleton is supposed to be my swan-song to the com colour interpretation of collage. I think, in a roundabout that might be my last screenprint. I want to get on to n more cottage-industry type prints which are much n studio-orientated.' (Paolozzi, quoted in St Andrews, 1979 spite of this statement Paolozzi has gone on to make fur screenprints, as well as wood engravings and etchings.

C3.26

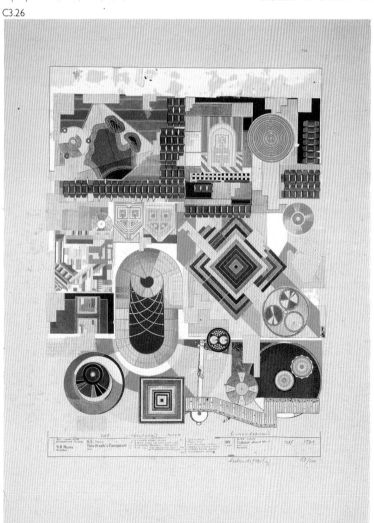

C3.27

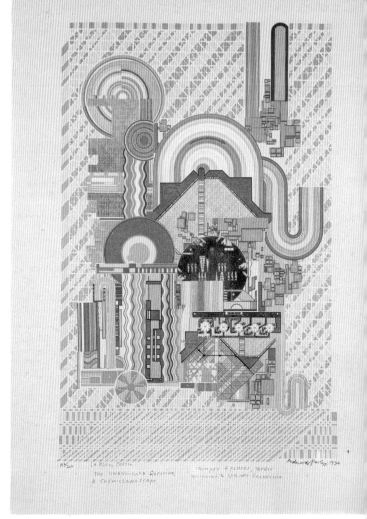

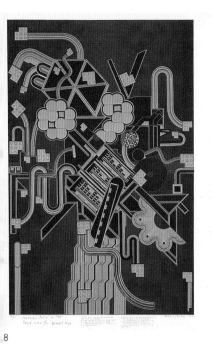

8

C3.29

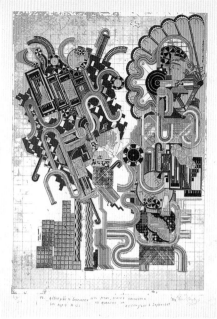

C3.30

I

C3.32

C3.33

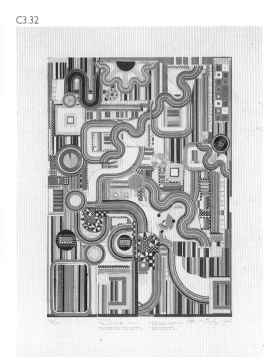

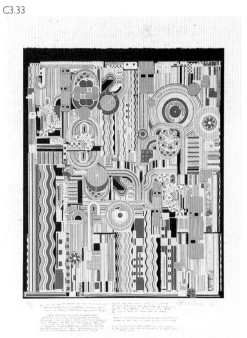

C3.35 Where Reality Lies

Screenprint with hand colouring, 1982
63 × 100
Exh. Oxford 1982

According to the artist, this work 'has a long history and like most prints I have made contains elements collected over a considerable period of time. These elements represent a metaphor. They may start life as a readymade, often found in the streets. For example the Chinese cigarette packet was discarded outside the Louvre and Christ was the wrapper of a book in the wastepaper basket of a keeper's room in a museum.' (Paolozzi, in 'Innovations in Contemporary Print-making' Oxford 1982).

C3.41

C3.36 Mr Machine

Etching, 1983
75.5 × 57/64.25 × 46

C3.37 Man One, Pig One

Etching, 1984
67.5 × 51/ 18.5 × 24.5 and 14.5 × 12.5
Edition of 5

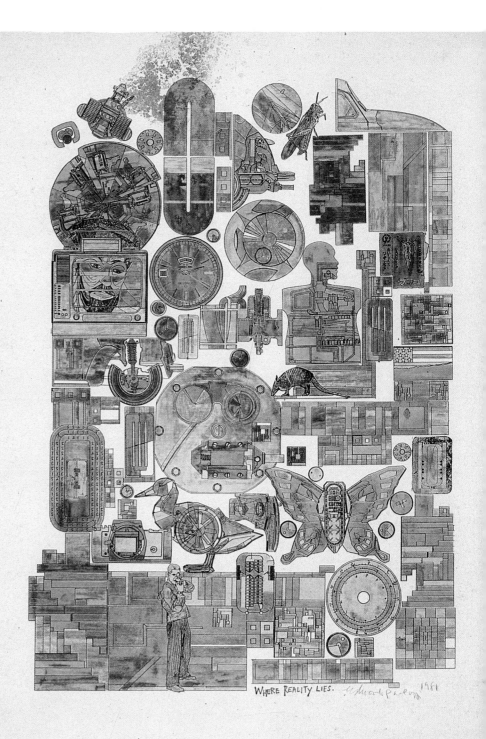

WHERE REALITY LIES.   1981

3.35

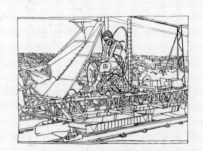

8 Man Two, Monkey One
ing, 1984
× 51/ 13.25 × 12.75 and 12.5 × 18.5   C3.37
on of 5

9 Falklands Figures   C3.38
ing, 1984
× 51/ 30.5 × 31.5
on of 5   C3.36

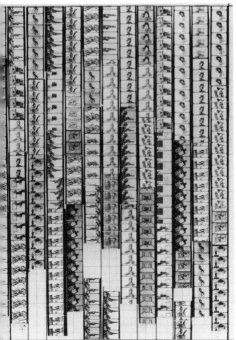

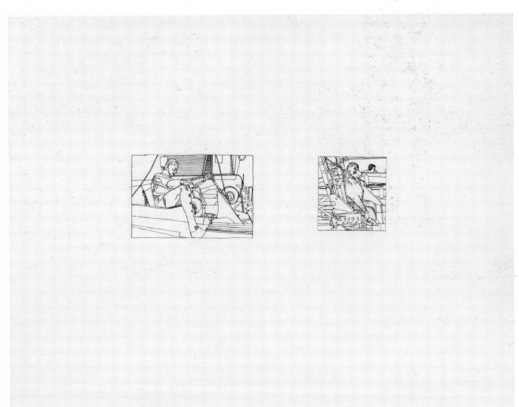

C3.40 **Running Man**

Etching, 1984
67.5 x 51/ 49.25 x 36.4
Edition of 5
The running man is a recurrent theme in Paolozzi's recent graphics, which relates to George Orwell's '1984'.

C3.41 **Figure I**

Woodcut, 1984
57 x 38
This print was printed at the Royal Academy School in May 1984.

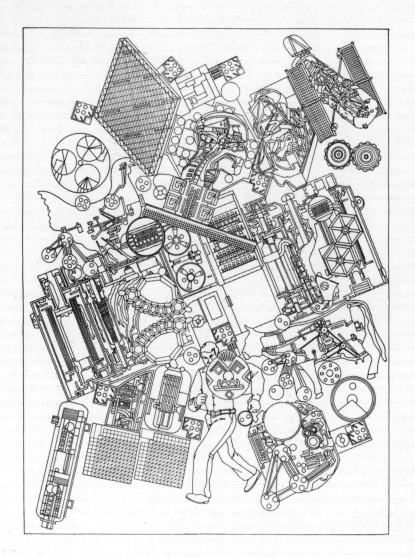

C3.40

STUDIO TO CITY SQUARE

I have some friends who are achitects who would not dream of using art works in their buildings. Yet for an artist, doing large sculpture and projects for achitects can be a positive experience. One is able to achieve something outside the studio, perhaps trying for something within new disciplines – something which would not be possible if one conducted one's artistic life in a totally private way. Also one is creating – and this is perhaps the role of great sculpture – certain kinds of monuments. In the great historic tradition the sculpture you make is for the public, to be enjoyed by the public. That is where the emphasis must be.

In any form of public art – designs for an underground station or sculpture in a city square – one knows that one is making a kind of bridge, contact with people on a massive scale. Many projects combining art with architecture would only be possible through the eduction and needs of those people. In this I think the architect must be the main catalyst.

EDUARDO PAOLOZZI
London 1984

Moorweidenstrasse relief

The steel frame of the Centre Beaubourg crisscrosses the nave of Cologne Cathedral; three girls astride a rocket pass a flying fish and a space man propels himself towards the Gothic vault. The Laocoön sits unincongruously beside Gothic and industrial styles of architecture.

The co-existence of such disparate styles might indicate an affiliation with a post-modernist aesthetic in architecture. Paolozzi's series of screenprints **Blueprints for a New Museum** 1980 (D3.18-24) symbolically acknowledge the liberating influence of recent architecture. The architect of the Centre Beaubourg has also acknowledged Paolozzi's influence,[1] and the artist is not unaware of the effect his work has had on changing styles in the last thirty years. Yet the mixing of styles, rather than a unified adherence to one, whether pre or post-modernist, has always characterised Paolozzi's approach to making art. A number of works he showed in his Tate Gallery exhibition in 1971, made specially for the occasion, were labelled 'conceptual', 'minimal', etc., and deliberately satirised the cataloguing mentality of art critics and the modern art world. Paolozzi's reluctance to be continually identified with 'Pop' is well known.

Nevertheless, Paolozzi's art does have affinities with post-war architecture, and over the years the surface treatment of his sculpture is reflected by current styles of architectural embellishment. His association with the architects Alison and Peter Smithson over the exhibition 'This is Tomorrow', at the ICA in 1956 did not result in sculpture commissions; but his 'art brut' style sculpture was paralelled by the rought cast finishes of 'New Brutalist' architecture to which the Smithsons made such important contributions in the early 1950's.[2] It is not so much a question of mutual influences, but of common sources of interest in the architecture and art movements of the 1920's and 1930's, which Paolozzi has shared with some of his architect friends such as James Stirling and Richard Rogers.

In 1976 Paolozzi spoke of his desire to breathe fresh life into the tradition of craftsmanship and design as represented by William Morris in England and Charles Rennie Mackintosh in Scotland.[3] References to Mackintosh as well

as to Frank Lloyd Wright are to be found in his prints, which o[...] significantly, in the more hand-made medium of woodcut and etc[...] (D3.8-11 & 25-27). Similarly, it is to Michelangelo as an architect, rather as a sculptor, that Paolozzi pays hommage in a screenprint (D3.7).

Instead of finding root in Britain, the traditions of craftsmanship and de[...] found more sympathetic translation in terms of the twentieth centu[...] Germany, at the Bauhaus in the 1920's. Maybe for Paolozzi it is fortu[...] that they did, for he has had a long association with Germany. If any de[...] this century holds more significance for him in art than another, it must s[...] be the decade of his birth, when artists and architects, stirred by[...] inhumanity of war, reacted to their surroundings by commenting, impro[...] and transcending them; and expressed themselves in a multitude of st[...] constructive, expressionist and surrealist.

Although Paolozzi has been closely associated with architects in the[...] he has recently expressed a reluctance to continue making public art, su[...] the mosaic decorations for Tottenham Court Road station in London. F[...] ancient times, decoration has been applied to buildings and walls. Only in[...] twentieth century, after Adolf Loos and functionalist theory, has the ide[...] decoration in architecture become a subject of aesthetic embarrassm[...]

Part of Paolozzi's dissatisfaction with making public art stems from[...] breakdown in craft traditions, which are always necessary if the artist's i[...] are to be satisfactorily translated into a permanent and durable form. I[...] ideas and concepts, conceived in private, and their manifestation in pu[...] can often become confused. The gap between the tradition of fine art[...] craft work is often unbridgeable. Although there are interesting[...] undeniable opportunities in doing work on a scale which canno[...] attempted in the studio, obsessions of a private nature are usually[...] explored on the smaller scale of etchings and drawings. They are ultim[...] more important for the artist if he is to make creative progress. Only ther[...] such 'laboratory' work in the field of fine art act as the stimulus or yea[...] make public statements.[4]

Such a process can best be demonstrated by the **Hommage à Bruck[...]** and **Camera** sculptures of 1977 and 1978-9 (D1.2 & D1.6), all conceive[...] a large scale. They were first worked out in smaller versions, parts of w[...] also cross-fertilize with the graphic imagery of the mid-1970s. Paolozz[...]

STUDIO TO CITY SQU[...]

age à Bruckner, installation

ished some of the source material for these works.[5] But underlying the
hitheatre-like associations of **Camera** and the related sculpture
amalla are Norman Bel Geddes's theatre designs of the mid-1920s,
oduced in Léon Moussinac's **Tendances Nouvelles du Théâtre**, a
y of which Paolozzi owns.[6]

he imagery of the **Calcium Light Night** screenprints of 1974-6
.26-34) is also rephrased in several public works such as the decoration
he Berlin Wall in 1976, the Monchengladbach **Wall Relief**, 1979 (B1.21)
the bronze relief for Moorweidenstrasse, Hamburg, 1979
18-19).

here is a special pleasure in perpetuating in art a motif or symbol from a
e ephemeral and fleeting medium, such as the cinema or the theatre,
Paolozzi is well aware of this potential. Like **Camera**, the **Piscator**
ture for Euston Square, London, also pays hommage to a great artist of
modern theatre, in this case the Expressionist director, Erwin Piscator. It
development and refinement of the so-called 'motor-bike' heads,
natively titled **Naked Head** and **Portrait of Matta**. The sculpture is
ded to be read from different points on the square, and can also be seen
viewpoints above ground level. Paolozzi welcomes different interpre-
ns of the work because he recognises that 'modern experience has
wn us that a specific object in a public space may appeal in a variety of
s'. For instance, its meaning can be subtly altered by the changing times of
or by the seasons. It was necessary to keep in mind not only the casual
er-by and the regular train commuter, but the large number of people
king in the building complex. Such careful social considerations are only
y evidenced in recent architecture, and indicate just how valuable the
t's contribution would be in removing drudgery and monotony from
ern buildings.[7]

While allowing others a certain flexibility in their interpretation, Paolozzi
a paradox between the sources and physical expression of **Piscator**,

because it relates to the subject of the portrait head which has obsessed him
for nearly forty years. 'With many ideas in art there exists a paradox and in
the cast of the Euston Head one has merged a theme which goes back to
antiquity – a man's head and shoulders – with a modern view of the way our
society is affected by the machine'.[8]

Dissatisfied with the centuries' old tradition of placing a sculpture in the
middle of a city plaza, but mindful of the many social meanings art can still
have, Paolozzi has devised a homogeneous scheme for the Rhinegarden,
Cologne, which meets the needs of the ever-expanding population of a large
twentieth-century European town. For this purpose he designed what he
has described as 'a quasi-mechanistic shape which can be sat upon, leaned
against and climbed upon. It appears as a spreading grouping of arranged
semi-objects curving forward and sideways and making connections with
Bischofsgartenstrasse (and from there with the Romanische Germanische
Museum). Each object is part of the whole yet is meant to be unique and
shared with the landscaping and the people'.[9]

The scheme was developed out of the decision to divert cars under the
Rhinegarden, so that the 'dissolving motor car' in its union with nature could
also become a motif/symbol for the design. Paolozzi sees this, like his reliefs,
in the context of musical expression. 'As in music the motif will be clearly
defined at the point of most concentration but will fall away into fragments of
pieces – yet individual elements positioned with care will pick out and repeat
those visual chords and occasional arpeggios'[10].

Rhinegarden project

Notes

1. Eduardo Paolozzi, **Private Vision – Public Art**, The Architectural
Association, London, 24 February – 31 March 1984, (exhibition catalogue)
p. 45.
2. See Rayner Banham, **The New Brutalism**, London, 1966.
3. Interview with Eduardo Paolozzi, BBC, Radio Scotland, June 1976.
4. Eduardo Paolozzi, BBC, Radio 3, March 1984.
5. Eduardo Paolozzi, **Work in Progress**, Kölnischer Kunstverein,
19 October – 11 November 1979, pp. 70-71, (exhibition catalogue).
6. 'Jeanne d'Arc de Mercedes de Agosta, décors, costumes et mise en scène
de Norman Bel Geddes, Théâtre de la Porte Sainte-Martin, Paris 1925',
plate 116 in Léon Moussinac, **Tendances Nouvelles du Théâtre**, Les
editions Albert Lévy, Paris 1931.
7. Eduardo Paolozzi, **Private Vision, Public Art**, 1984, p.26.
8. **Ibid**.
9. **Ibid**. p.40
10. **Ibid**.

DIO TO CITY SQUARE

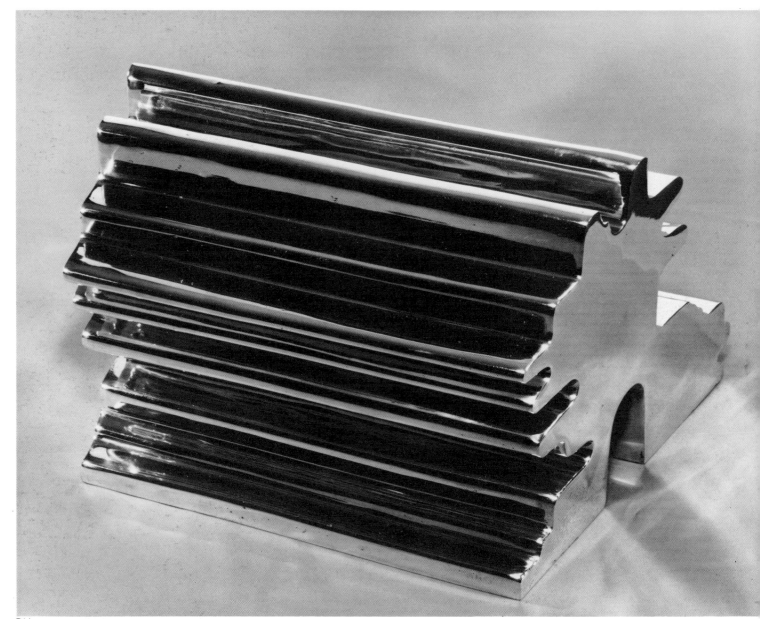

D1.1

D1.1 **Osaka Steel**

Polished bronze, 1969

59 × 40 × 40

Exh: London 1971 (58); Berlin 1975 (53)

Lit: Kirkpatrick 1970 p. 83 repr. pl. 50 (finished sculpture in situ); Whitford 1971 p. 17 repr. p. 16 (finished sculpture in situ); Konnertz 1984 pp. 154, 156 repr. pl. 303 (finished sculpture in situ).

This work was the result of an invitation to a group of sculptors from Europe and America to produce steel sculpture in collaboration with the Japanese steel industry. It thus represents a continuation of the co-operation between sculptor and factory which Paolozzi had established with C.W. Juby Ltd., in England.

DI.3 **Matamalla**

Bronze, sd. 'Eduardo Paolozzi 1979'
4 × 28 × 23
Exh: St Andrews 1979 (61) Ediburgh 1979 (174) repr.
pl. 11
Lit: Cologne 1979 repr. p. 72; Konnertz 1984 p. 238 repr.
pl. 433
Relates to Camera (See Cat. DI.6).
See Plate XXI

DI.4 **Matamalla**

Plaster, 1979
4 × 28 × 23
Lit: Cologne 1979 repr. p. 72 Konnertz 1984 repr. pl. 428
Relates to Camera (See Cat. DI.6).

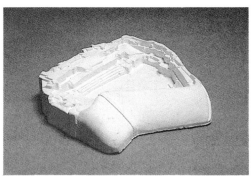

DI.4

DI.5 **Matamalla**

Bronze, sd 'E.Paolozzi',1979
54 × 41 × 11
Edition of 3
Exh: Edinburgh 1979 (175)
Relates to **Camera** (DI.6)

Hommage à Bruckner

r.
25 × 8
Cologne 1979 repr. (also related graphic work and
graph of the installation of the sculpture); London 1984
8-19; Konnertz 1984 p. 237 repr. pl. 424
a study for a large sculpture in cast iron, for Linz, Austria,
ally commissioned for the Exhibition 'Forum Metall'. As
he graphic series **Ravel Suite** and **Calcium Light Night**,
eaning of the work is dependent upon a dedication to a
oser, and is not intended as an illustration to Bruckner's
.

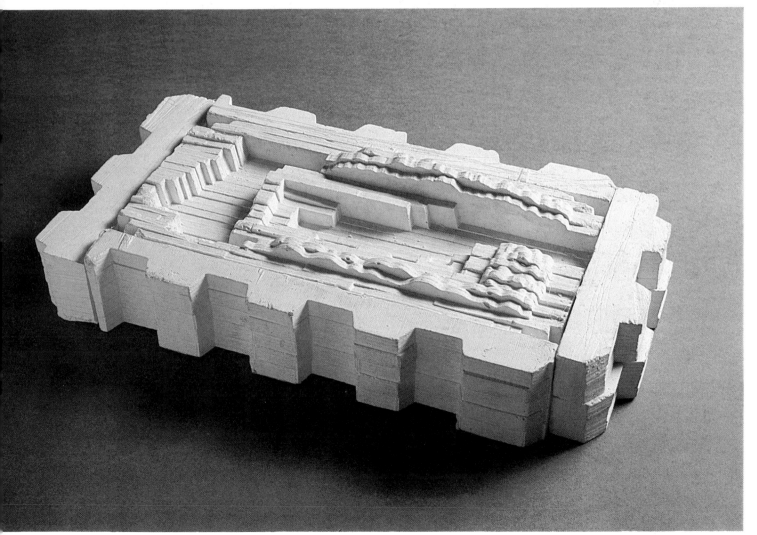

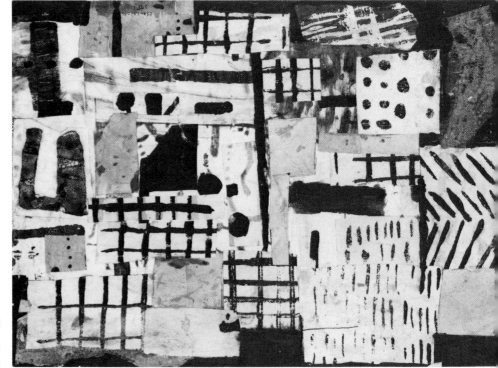

D2.1

D1.6 Maquette for Camera
Resin and wood, 1979
6.25 cm high on wood base 34.5 × 35
Lit: London 1984 pp. 20-21 repr. of study and finished sculpture in situ; Konnertz 1984 pp. 235, 237ff, 243, 255. Source material for **Camera** is reproduced in Cologne 1979 pp. 70-71 and Konnertz 1984 pls. 426, 431, 432. It includes an illustration of the cross-section of the interior of a polaroid camera, and photographs of an open-cast goldmine and an archaeological reconstruction of a village in New Mexico.

Camera was commissioned for the European Patent Office in Munich after a closed international sculpture competition. It is cast in iron in nine elements and is situated outside the building at the convergence of two streets. Its open design and proximity to a public pathway encourages people to enter the sculpture.

D2.1 Untitled
Collage and pen, sd 'Eduardo Paolozzi 1951'
28.5 × 41
Lit: Sotheby's 1983 (299) repr.
Originally a gift to the architects Jane Drew and Maxwell Fry. The design is similar to a large collage mural which Paolozzi created for their office (repr. Kirkpatrick 1970 pl. 29).

D2.2 Untitled
Collage, gouache and screenprint, sd 'Eduardo Paolozzi 1957'
50.5 × 76
Exh: A.C.G.B. (touring exh.) 1965 'The Maxwell Fry – Jane Drew Collection.'
Lit: Sotheby's 1983 (301) repr.
Originally a gift from the artist to Maxwell Fry and Jane Drew. It is similar to a screenprinted ceiling design by Paolozzi of 1952, commissioned through the architect Sir Ove Arup.

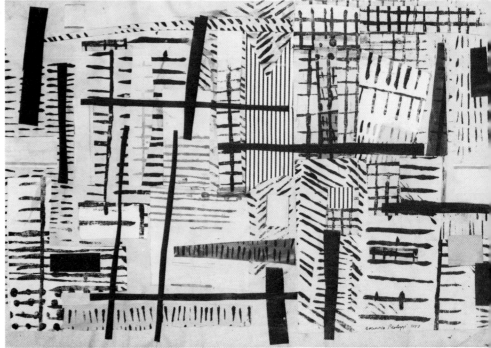

D2.2

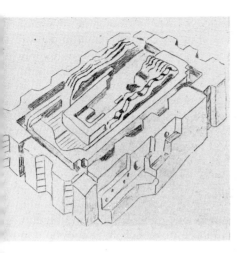

Hommage à Bruckner
I, 1977
62
Cologne 1979 repr. p. 73; Konnertz 1984 p. 237 repr.
23
dy for the sculpture **Hommage à Bruckner**, 1977, cast
n (6 × 5 × 0.8 metres) situated ouside the Brucknerhaus,
Austria (see D1.2).

Hommage à Bruckner
I, 1977
62

Detail of Camera
I, 1979
56

Detail of Camera
I, 1979
56

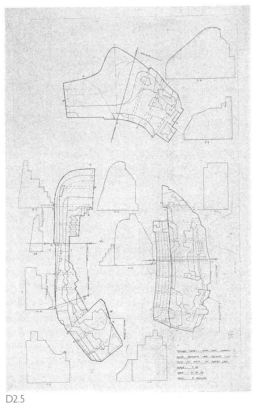

D2.5

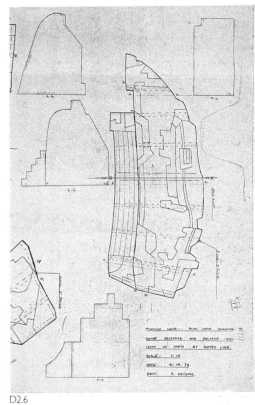

D2.6

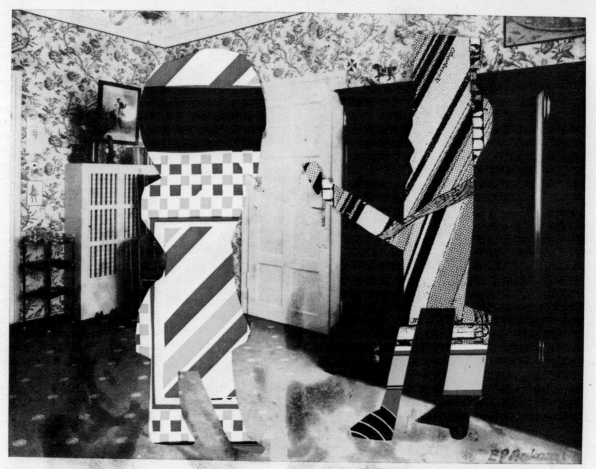

ARCHITEKT K. J. MOSSNER u. P. HULDSCHINSKY. ANKLEIDEZIMMER DES HERRN.

D2.7 **Architect K.J. Mossner**
Collage
21.25 x 29.5

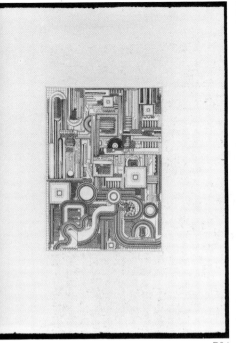

I-6 **The Ravel Suite**
es of six etchings, 1974
ion of 15
3 × 38.1 (sheet size) : various plate sizes
ranjuex 25.5 × 18.4
Ci Boure 25.4 × 20.3
Die Versunkene Glocke 22.4 × 16.2
eux d'eau 25.4 × 14.7

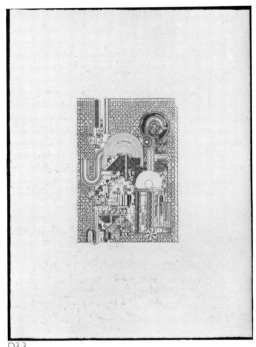

D3.2
5. Zaspiak Bat 25.4 × 19.3
6. Olympia 25.3 × 16.2
Lit: London 1977 p. 48 (164-169) ; Konnertz 1984 pp. 202, 215, 217ff, 225, 226, 229, 233, 246, 261 repr. pls. 394, 395, 398, 400.
In the mid-1970s, Paolozzi began to turn to music as a source for his graphic works. His abstract imagery became a visual

D3.3
equivalent of musical ideas and forms. This set of etchings reflects the refined character of Ravel's music, each print taking its title and inspiration from a work by Ravel. 'Jeux d'eau', for example, is one of Ravel's major works which the composer has described as 'inspired by the sound of water and music of fountains, it is founded on two motifs after the fashion of the first movement of a sonata, without, however, being subjected to the classical plan.'

D3.5

D3.6

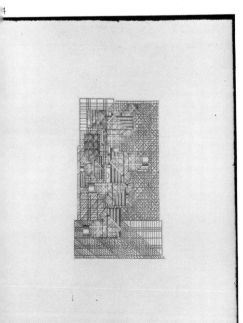

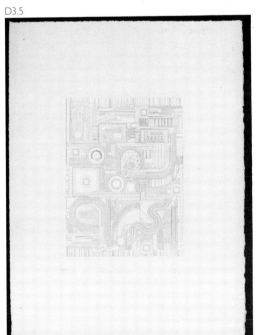

D3.7 Omaggio a Michelangelo

Etching and photogravure, printed from two copper plates, 1975
80 × 59/58.6 × 49.2
Edition of 200
The image is based on one of Michelangelo's unrealised architectural drawings.

D3.8-11 For Charles Rennie Mackintosh

Set of 6 Woodcuts, 1975
64.9 × 65.4/40 × 40
Edition of 20 and 20 artists proofs
 8. Sobotka
 9. Pryde-Pierrot
10. Lead Cameron
11. Ard King Las
12. For the Four
13. Eros the Dresser
Lit: London 1977 pp. 53, 56 (194-199); Konnertz 1984 pp. 225ff, 234. repr. pls. 407,408.

In contrast to the precision of his screenprint images in the **Calcium Light Night** suite of 1974-6 (C3.26-34), Paolozzi here turns to a coarser line with the more traditional technique of woodcut. His use of strong linear elements and chequered patterns reflects Mackintosh's own vocabulary, but it is clearly related to the style Paolozzi had developed in previous graphics such as the **Ravel Suite** of 1974 The titles refer to Mackintosh and his contemporaries:- Sobotka: Adolf Loos (1870-1933) designed a bedroom for Walter Sabot 1902, which can be compared with Mackintosh's bedro design at Mains Street, Glasgow (1900). 'Pryde-Pierro drawing entitled 'Pierrot', dated 1897 by James Pryde. W by Pryde appeared in Charles Hiatt's survey of contempo poster design 'Picture Posters' of 1895, a possible sourc inspiration for 'The Four'. Mackintosh and Pryde later bec good friends. Lead Cameron: The name of a hous Bearsden, Glasgow, whose interiors were designed George Walton. Walton (1867-1933) was a contempo of Mackintosh, but they worked independently and their w has little in common. Ard King Las: 'Ardkinglaass' was name of a house in Argyllshire, designed by Sir Robert Lori 1906-08. For the Four: 'The Four' was the title given Mackintosh, Herbert MacNair and the Macdonald sis whilst at the Glasgow School of Art in the 1890s. Eros Dresser: 'Eros' was the title given to a large mosaic p designed by George Walton for the 1901 Glasgow In national Exhibition, and related in style to Mackintosh's w Christopher Dresser (1834-1904) was a professi designer for industrial production.

D3.7

D3.27

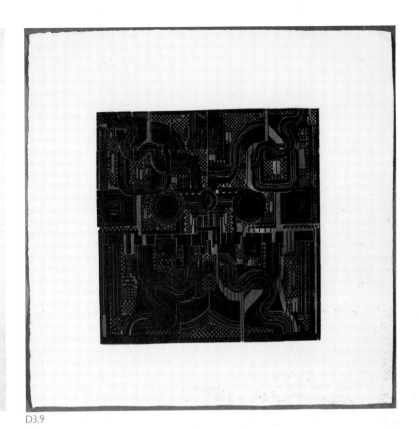

D3.9

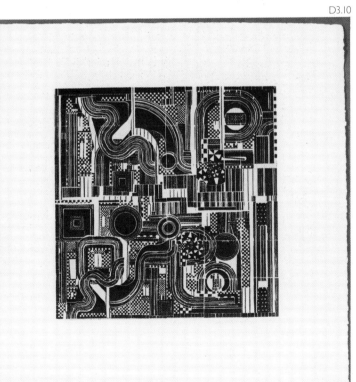

D3.10

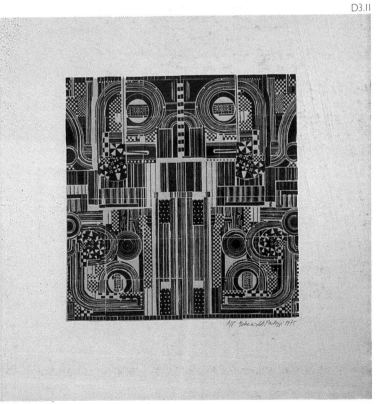

D3.11

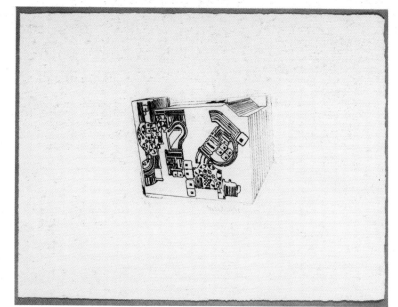

D3.12

D3.12 **Study of Berlin Wall**
Woodcut, 1976
9.5 x 13/25 x 33

D3.13 **Hommage à Bruckner**
Etching, 1977
22.75 x 29
See D2.3 and D2.4.

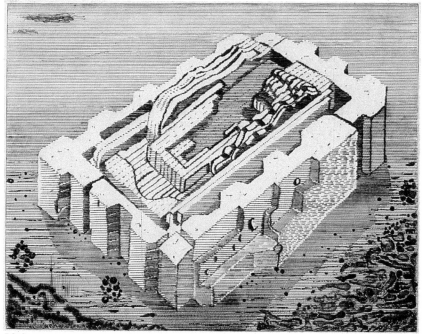

D3.13

D4.1

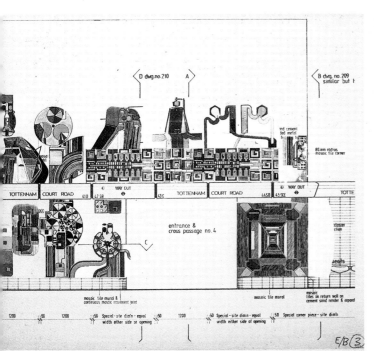

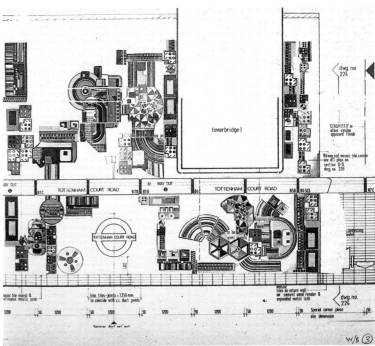

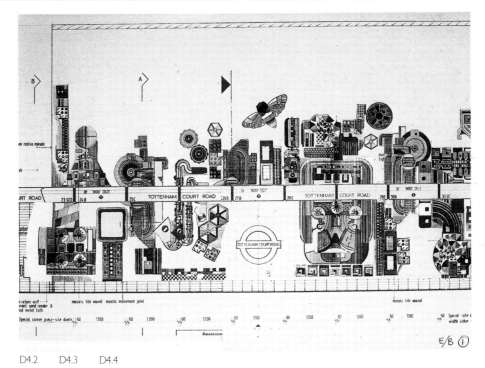

D4.2   D4.3   D4.4

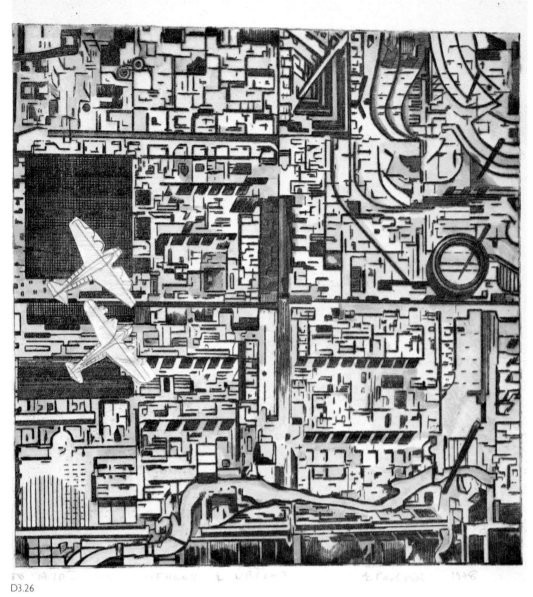

D3.26

D3.16

D3.14 **Parkplatz**
Etching, 1979
34 × 48.5
The illustration shows the model used as a basis for the etchings.

D3.15 **Parkplatz**
Etching, hand-coloured, 1979
26 × 35.5

D3.16 **Camera**
Relief print, sd 'Eduardo Paolozzi 79'
14 × 9/27 × 18
Private collection

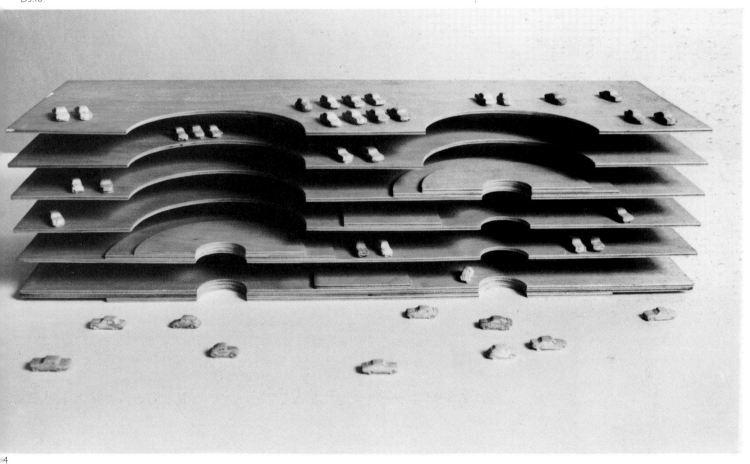

D3.17 Viernes Sabado

Screenprint 1979
66 × 57.5
Lit: Konnertz 1984 pp. 256,266,268 repr. pls. 465-8

D3.18-23 Mein Kolner Dom – Blueprints for a New Museum

Set of six stage lithographs and screenprints, 1980-81
75 × 63
Exh: Cologne 1980 (repr. pp. 120-23); Berlin 1983-4 (repr.)
Lit: Paolozzi 1983 pp. 41, 42 repr. fig. 6; Konnertz 1984 pp. 250ff, 257 repr. pls. 455,456.

For these prints Paolozzi used transparent film to 'float' the images on top of each other. His work was part of a project, in which other artists participated, to celebrate the centenary of the completion of the spire of Cologne Cathedral. He records 'I created a kind of blueprint for my ideal museum – the museum has one example of everything that is wonderful and has meaning – an aeroplane, railway engine, a large model of a pig, Einstein, computers, the Beaubourg.' (Paolozzi 1983).

D3.24 Blueprint for a New Museum

Stone lithograph and screenprint, 1981
75 × 63
Commissioned by Gail Tiles as a promotional gift.

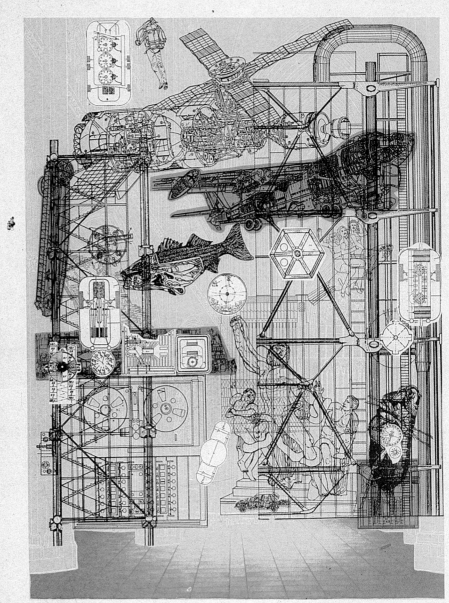

Blueprints for a New Museum

D3.24

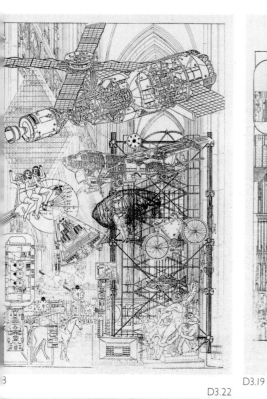

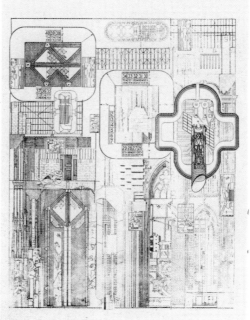

D3.22

D3.19

D3.23

D3.21

D3.20

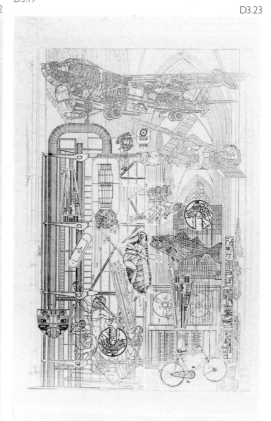

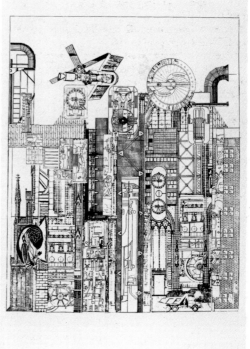

D3.25 **Study for Utopia**
Etching with hand coloured collage, 1983
75 x 57
Exh: Oxford 1982
Of this series of studies, Paolozzi has written: 'The background landscape is based on Frank Lloyd Wright's model for Broadacre City. This might represent a scheme with political undertones. Above the basic pattern fly three aeroplanes which refer simultaneously to several ideas – a notion of space and a hint of autobiography.' (Paolozzi, in 'Innovations in Contemporary Printmaking', Oxford 1982).

D3.26 **Study for Utopia**
Etching with hand coloured collage, 1983
75 x 57
Exh: Oxford 1982
See Plate XXIV

D3.27 **F.L.W.**
Etching, 1984
67.5 x 51 / 36.5 x 35.75
Edition of 5

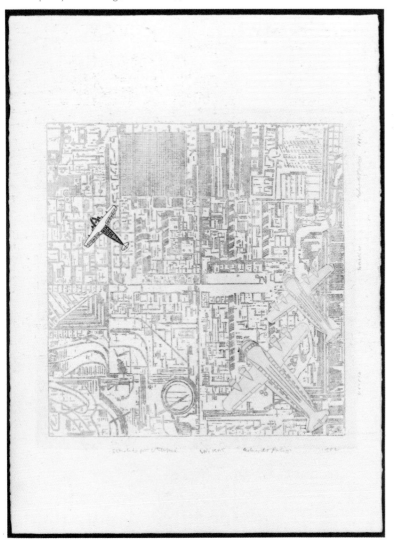

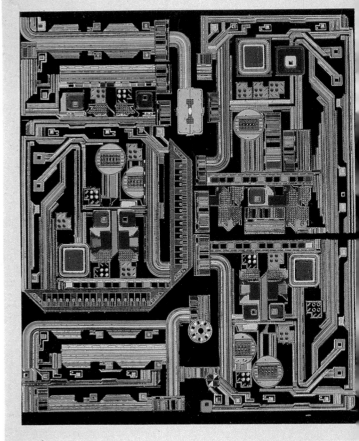

D3.17

.I Working Model for Glasgow University Doors

ale 1:6)
od 1976
3 × 63.5 × 26
n: Edinburgh 1976 (19); St Andrews 1979 (55);
nburgh 1979 (170);
London 1984 p. 16/17 repr.; Paolozzi 1983 p. 44;
nnertz 1984 pp. 227, 237, 240, 269 repr. pl. 415.
e Glasgow University Doors were commissioned through
nitfield Partners, and installed in the Hunterian Gallery in
0. The panels were cast in aluminium at an Edinburgh
ndry and mounted on tubular steel frames hung in an
ening of tooled white granite concrete. Each door
asures 365.7 × 91.4cms. The imagery of the doors relates
hat of the **Berlin Wall** project of 1976 (see London 1984
4), the **Ravel Suite** (D3.1-6) and other graphic work of
mid-1970s. Paolozzi draws a comparison between the
nnique he used to create the images in an untitled etching
976 and his preparatory designs for the Glasgow doors.

The image for the etching was derived by cutting elements
from previous screenprints which were then moved around
to create new configurations. Similarly the doors were first
designed using plaster elements collaged on wooden boards.
(See Paolozzi 1983 p. 44.)
See Plate XXII

D4.2-5 Tottenham Court Road Tube Station Mosaics
Source material for Mosaic designs , dated from June 1981 to
May 1982.
Printed paper, Xerox, collage, hand-coloured elements
Various sizes
Lit: Paolozzi 1983 p. 41; London 1984 pp. 32:33 reprs.;
Konnertz 1984 pp. 246ff reprs.
Paolozzi has made extensive use of xerox as a means of
altering the colour and size of original collages, and found it an
essential technique to cope with a design project of this size.
The mosaics were commissioned by London Transport,
Department of Architecture and Design for the entrance
area, passages and platforms of Tottenham Court Road Tube
Station. The character of Paolozzi's designs, although varied
unifies the different areas of the station, providing the unique
'station identity' stressed by the Department. The panels are
formed from 22m square glass units and irregular 'smalti'.
See Plate XXIII for some of the finished designs.

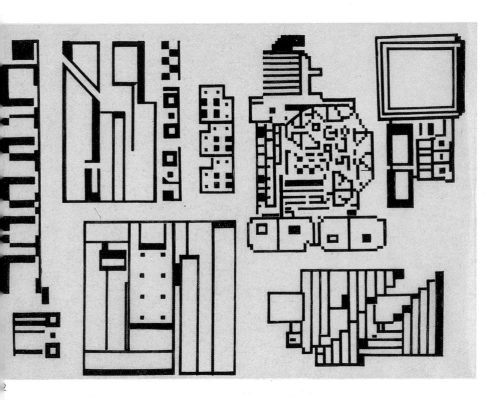

2

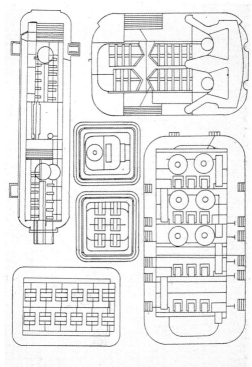

D4.3

D4.6 Model for Pesch Playground, Cologne
Wood, 1982
30 x 60 x 20
Lit: London 1984 p. 42 repr. Konnertz 1984 p. 254 pl. 463.

Model for a playground in cast aluminium, commissioned by the City of Cologne. Like **Rhino** (B1.22), it provides children with a means of exploring an art object by touch as much as by sight.

The work was constructed in a German factory from various ready made aluminium elements: it could perhaps therefore be seen in the context of Paolozzi's still-life sculptures such as **Mechanik's Bench** (C1.11), inspired by the components of his machine sculptures awaiting assembly.

D4.6

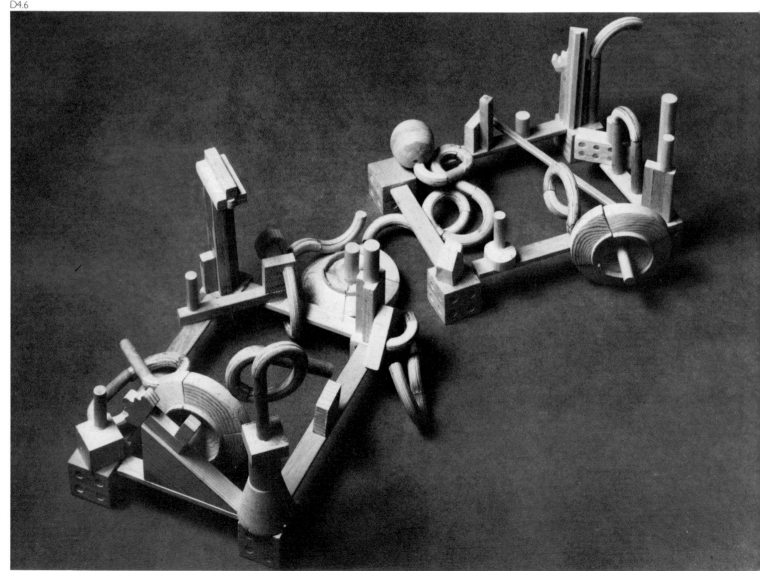

e from a scrapbook.
umber of scrapbook pages, selected by the artist, will be
ided in the exhibition.

FURTHER READING
& LOOKING

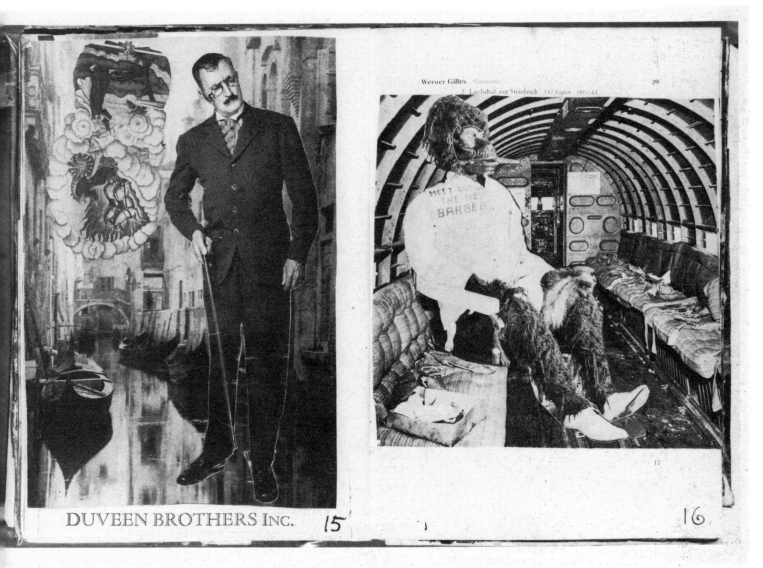

CHRONOLOGY

1924 7 March: Born, Leith, Edinburgh, son of Rudolfo and Carmella Paolozzi of Viticuso, Frosinone, Italy.

1930s Attends annual summer camps in Italy

1940 Interned under Emergency Powers Act and spends three months in gaol. Death of father when ship 'Arandora Star is torpedoed in Atlantic.

1943 Attends evening classes at Edinburgh College of Art with ambitions to become a commercial artist

June: enlisted in Royal Pioneer Corps; stationed at Slough and Windsor.

1944 14 September: Discharged from Pioneer Corps; Attends St Martin's School of Art, London.

1945-7 Attends Slade School of Art, evacuated to Oxford during the war; enrols in sculpture class;

Spends some nights on firewatch in the Ashmolean Museum; makes drawings after African sculpture in the Pitt Rivers Museum. Friendships with Nigel Henderson, Raymond Mason and William Turnbull.

1946-7 Living in Cartwright Gardens, London.

1947 First exhibition at the Mayor Gallery, London

Summer: leaves for Paris

13 October: enrols briefly at the Ecole des Beaux-Arts

1947-9 Living in Paris; addresses include Rue Bade and Rue Visconti; meets Jean Arp, Braque, Brancusi, Giacometti, Jean Hélion, Léger, Mary Reynolds and Tristian Tazara. Léger arranges for Paolozzi to see his film 'Ballet Mécanique'

Absorbs Surrealist ideas and sees Dubuffet's 'art brut'

1949 Returns to London; lives in Bethnal Green and Shepherd's Bush where he shares a studio with William Turnbull. Often sees Francis Bacon.

1949-55 Teaches Textile Design at Central School of Art and Design

1950 Screenprinting experiments at London College of Printing and at the Central School with Anton Ehrenzweig.

1951 Married Freda Elliot.

Commissioned to make fountain for Festival of Britain South Bank site

1952 Commissioned through Sir Ove Arup and Alison and Peter Smithson to design ceiling decoration for the offices of R.S.Jenkins, 8 Fitzroy Street, London.

Member of the Independent Group at the Institute of Contemporary Arts; gives lecture 'Bunk' and in it shows his early collages which leads to discussion on the symbolism of popular imagery and differences between British and American popular culture.

British Critics' Prize

1953 Organises the exhibition 'Parallel of Life and Art' at the Institute of Contemporary Arts, with Nigel Henderson, Ronald Jenkins, Alison and Peter Smithson. Paolozzi shows photographs of machines, paintings and drawings to illustrate the unity of artistic and scientific information.

Finalist in competition for 'Unknown Political Prisoner' sponsored by the Contemporary Art Society;

Commissioned to make fountains for International Horticultural Exhibition, Hamburg.

1954 Daughter Louise Carmella born

1955-58 Teaches sculpture at St Martin's School of Art

1955 Starts 'Hammer Prints' with Nigel Henderson, to produce and market designs for textiles, wallpaper and ceramics.

1956 Collaborated on section 6, 'Patio and Pavilion', of the exhibition 'This is Tomorrow' at the Whitechapel Art Gallery, London, with Nigel Henderson, and Alison and Peter Smithson

1956 Norma and Wiliam Copley Foundation Award

1956 Starred in film 'Together' by Lorenza Mazetti

1957 Daughter Anna Francisca born

1960 Award for the Best Sculptor under 45 given by the David E Bright Foundation at the 30th Venice Biennale.

Daughter Emma Naomi born

1960-2 Visiting Professor to advise on sculpture and basic design at Stattliche Hochschule fur bildende Kunste, Hamburg.

1961 Watson F. Blair Prize at 64th Annual American Exhibition, Chicago.

1962 Makes screenprints with Christopher Prater, Kelpra Studios.

On return from Hamburg begins association with C.W.Juby, Engineering, Ipswich. 'British Art Today' tours America.

1967 Purchase Prize, International Sculpture Exhibition, Solomon R. Guggenheim Museum, New York.

First Prize for Sculpture, Carnegie International Exhibition of Contemporary Painting and Sculpture, Pittsburgh.

1968 C.B.E.

Visiting Professor Art, University of California, Berkeley

1968 Begins teaching in Ceramics Department, Royal College of Art

1969 Makes sculpture for Expo Osaka, and lives in Japan

1971 Retrospective exhibition at Tate Gallery, London

1975 Saltire Society Award for ceiling panels and window tapestry at Cleish Castle, Scotland.

1974-5 Lives and works in Berlin as guest of Deutschen Akademischen Austauschdienstes (DAAD)

1975 Retrospective exhibition at Nationalgalerie, Berlin; complete prints exhibited at Kupferstichkabinett

1976 Commission for wall decoration at Kurfurstenstrasse 87, West Berlin.

Commission for doors for Hunterian Art Gallery, Glasgow University.

1977-81 Appointed Professor of Ceramics at Fachhochschule, Fachbereich Kunst und Desin, Cologne.

1977 Commission for 'Hommage à Anton Bruckner' for exhibition Forum Metall, Linz, Austria.

Complete prints exhibited at the Victoria and Al Museum.

1978 Commission for 'Camera', European Patent Of Munich in closed scupture competition.

1979 Commission for Wall Relief by City of Monch gladbach;

Royal Academician, London.

Birth of grandaughter Ella

Private commission of bronze relief triptych for Moorweic strasse 3, Hamburg

Honorary Doctorate, Royal College of Art

1980 Commission for 'Piscator' by British Rail, Euston Squ London;

Commission for Tottenham Court Road Tube Sta mosaics by London Transport;

Honorary Doctor of Literature, Glasgow University

Commission for Deutsch Welle Mosaics Head Of Cologne;

First prize in closed competition for development of Rh garten in Cologne.

1981 Commission of tapestry triptych for Great Hall, Insti of Chartered Accountants, London.

Commission by Redditch Development Corporation fo glass mosaic panels in Milward Square, Kingfisher Shop Centre – officially opened by HM The Queen 1983.

Made Honorary Member, Architectural Associa London.

Appointed Professor of Sculpture at Akademie der bilden Kunste, Munich;

Saltire Society Award for Aluminium Relief Doors of H terian Gallery, University of Glasgow.

1981-2 Professor of Master Class, Internationale Somr akademie für bildende Kunste, Salzburg, Austria;

Cast aluminium playground, commissioned for Pesch Sc Cologne;

1982 Commissioned for fountain for Marden Exhibitio Berlin 1985

1983 Grand Prix d'Honneur, 15th International Print B nale, Ljubljana, Yugoslavia.

1984 Elected to Council of Architectural Associat London;

RTHER READING AND LOOKING

a detailed bibliography see Konnertz 1984, pp. 283-7)

ozzi was recently asked for a brief selection of books he
ght, for a variety of reasons, as being inspirational. First on
st came Ozenfant's **Foundations** which he knew from an
date.

nfant, **Foundations of Modern Art**, 1931 (Dover
).
uhemann and E.M. Kemp, **The Artist at Work**, Penguin
s, (Modern Painters series), 1951.
ndarbauten Frühe Astronomische Grossgeräte Aus
en Mexico und Peru, (exh. cat.), Munich 1976.
er's Circus, Whitney Museum of American Art, New

amorphoses in Nineteenth-Century Sculpture,
bridge, Mass. Fogg Art Museum, 1975.
sen, **Rodin's Gates of Hell**, Minneapolis, University of
esota Press, 1960.
sen, **Rodin Rediscovered**, Washington, 1981.
logue of Plaster Casts, Gipsoteca Vallardi, Milan, n.d.
clopédie Diderot (sculpture section particularly).

KS BY PAOLOZZI
afisikal Translations, Kelpra Studio Limited, London,
.

Metallization of a Dream, notes by the Sculptor and
by Lawrence Alloway, Lion and Unicorn Press, Royal
ge of Art, London, 1963.
edited by Richard Hamilton, Percy Lund Humphries for
William and Norma Copley Foundation, London,

a Zabba, edited and printed by Hansjorg Mayer and
nts at Watford School of Art, 1970.

CTION OF TEXTS, INTERVIEWS,
TEMENTS
amorphosis of Rubbish – Mr Paolozzi Explains his
ess', **The Times**, 2 May, 1958.
es from a Lecture at the Institute of Contemporary Arts,
, **Uppercase** (ed. Theo Crosby), London, 1958.
Ballard and Frank Whitford, 'Speculative Illustrations',
rview with Eduardo Paolozzi), **Studio International**,
ber, 1971.

Eduardo Paolozzi, 'The Iconongraphy of the Present', **Times
Literary Supplement**, 8 December, 1972.
'Eduardo Paolozzi – Bunk – The artist talking at an interview',
Victoria and Albert Museum, n.d. (1974).
'Eduardo Paolozzi über Piero di Cosimo' and 'Paolozzi über
Paolozzi' in **Kunstmagazin**, Nr. 81, 1978.
Eduardo Paolozzi, 'Junk and the New Arts and Crafts
Movement', in **Eduardo Paolozzi, Collages, Prints, Sculp-
tures**, Edinburgh University, Talbot Rice Art Centre, Edin-
burgh 1979 (exh. cat.).
Eduardo Paolozzi, 'The ad images that inspire today's artists', in
Campaign, 12 November, 1982.

BOOKS ON PAOLOZZI
Diane Kirkpatrick, **Eduardo Paolozzi**, London, 1970.
Winfried Konnertz, **Eduardo Paolozzi**, Cologne, 1984.
Michael Middleton, **Eduardo Paolozzi** ('Art in Progress'
series), London, 1963.
Uwe M. Schneede, **Paolozzi**, Stuttgart and New York,
1970.

BOOKS AND ARTICLES
Anton Ehrenzweig, **The Hidden Order of Art**, London,
1970.
British Sculpture in the Twentieth Century (ed. Nairne &
Serota), Whitechapel Art Gallery, London, 1981 (ex. cat.).
Christopher Finch, 'Paolozzi in the Sixties', **Art International**,
Vol. X, 1966.
Christopher Finch, **Image as Language, Aspects of British
Art 1950-1968**, Penguin, 1969.
Edward Gage, **The Eye in the Wind, Scottish Painting since
1945**, London, 1977.
Pat Gilmour, **Kelpra Studio, The Rose and Chris Prater
Gift, Artists' Prints 1961-1980**, The Tate Gallery, London,
1980.
Rosemary Miles, **The Complete Prints of Eduardo Paolozzi
– Prints, Drawings, Collages 1944-77**, Victoria and Albert
Museum, London, 1977.
Herbert Read, **The Art of Sculpture**, New York, 1956.
Karl Ruhrberg, 'Rendez-vous with Paolozzi' in **Eduardo**

Paolozzi, Recent Work, Fruitmarket Gallery, Edinburgh,
1976 (exh. cat.).
John Russell and Suzi Gablik, **Pop Art Redefined**, New York
and Washington, 1969.
William C. Seitz, **The Art of Assemblage**, New York,
1961.
Peter Selz, **New Images of Man**, New York, 1959.
Alison and Peter Smithson, 'But Tomorrow we Collect Ads',
in **Ark**, No. 18, Royal College of Art, 1957.
C.H. Waddington, **Behind Appearance**, A study of the
relations between painting and the natural sciences in this
century, Edinburgh, 1969.

FILMS BY PAOLOZZI
The History of Nothing, 1960-62, (with Denis Postle).
Kakafon Kakkoon, 1965 (Animation: Peter Leake and Keith
Griffiths).
Mr. Machine, 1971 (Animation: Peter Leake and Keith
Griffiths).
Λ8ΘI – Music for Modern Americans, 1983 (Animation:
Susan Young, Emma Clader, Isabelle Perrichon; Music: Stuart
Jones).

FILMS ABOUT PAOLOZZI
The Paolozzi Story, 1980, Al Lauder and Christiane
Waldbauer.
The Making of Piscator, 1982, Murray Grigor.

FILMS WITH PAOLOZZI
Together, Dir. Lorenza Mazetti, 1956.

SELECTED ONE MAN EXHIBITIONS

* Indicates catalogue published

Exhibition lists adapted, with permission, from W. Konnertz, Eduardo Paolozzi, Dumant, Cologne, 1984.

1947 Drawings and Sculptures by Eduardo Paolozzi. London, The Mayor Gallery, 14 January-1 February

1948 Eduardo Paolozzi – An Exhibition of Recent Drawings. London, The Mayor Gallery, 3-21 February

1949 Eduardo Paolozzi – Drawings and bas-Reliefs. London, The Mayor Gallery, 10-31 May

1957 Eduardo Paolozzi/Nigel Henderson. Cambridge, The Arts Council Gallery, 28 February-16 March

1958 Paolozzi Sculpture. London, Hanover Gallery, 11 November-31 December*

1960 Eduardo Paolozzi. New York, Betty Parsons Gallery, 14 March-2 April

1961 Victor Pasmore/Eduardo Paolozzi. Oslo, Kunstnernes Hus, 9 December-1 January 1962

1962 Paolozzi. New York, Betty Parsons Gallery, 23 April-12 May.

1963 Eduardo Paolozzi, New Works. London, The Waddington Galleries, 5-28 September*

1964 Eduardo Paolozzi: Recent Sculpture and Collage. London, Robert Fraser Gallery, 15 September-18 October*

Eduardo Paolozzi: Sculpture. New York, The Museum of Modern Art, 21 September-10 November*

Paintings of Alan Davie and Sculptures and Graphic Arts of Eduardo Paolozzi. Rio de Janeiro, Museu de Arte Moderna, 16 January-16 February

1965 Eduardo Paolozzi: Recent Sculptures, Drawings and Collages. Newcastle-upon-Tyne, Hatton Gallery, 8 February-6 March*

Eduardo Paolozzi: Sculptures, Collages, Graphics. London, Gallery of Chelsea School of Art, 3-26 May

Eduardo Paolozzi, 'As is When'. London, Editions Alecto, 4 May-25 June

1966 Eduardo Paolozzi: Recent Sculpture. New York, Pace Gallery, 2 January-2 February*

Eduardo Paolozzi: Sculpture, Prints. Edinburgh, Scottish National Gallery of Modern Art, 9 April-8 May

1967 Eduardo Paolozzi. Otterlo, Rijksmuseum Kröller-Müller, 7 May-2 July (with Anthony Caro)*

Eduardo Paolozzi: Sculpture and Graphics. London, Hanover Gallery, 14 June-21 July*

Eduardo Paolozzi, A Selection of Works from 1963-1966. London, Robert Fraser Gallery, Summer; New York, Pace Gallery, 18 November-16 December*

1968 Eduardo Paolozzi: A Print Retrospective. Berkeley, Worth Ryder Art Gallery, University of California, 15 May-9 June*

Eduardo Paolozzi: Serigrafieën. Amsterdam, Stedelijk Museum, Prentenkabinet, 24 May-30 June*

Paolozzi. London, Hanover Gallery*

Eduardo Paolozzi, Plastik und Graphik. Düsseldorf, Städtische Kunsthalle, 19 November-1 January 1969*

1969 Eduardo Paolozzi, An Exhibition of Original Sculpture, Gouaches, Drawings, Prints and enlarged black and white Photographs, Göteborg, Kunstmuseum, 20 September-19 October*

Eduardo Paolozzi, Complete Graphics. Berlin, Galerie Mikro*

Eduardo Paolozzi, Plastiken, Graphik. Hamburg, Kunsthaus, 5 April-18 May*

Society of Scottish Artists, Edinburgh

1971 Eduardo Paolozzi. London, The Tate Gallery, 22 September-31 October*

1972 Eduardo Paolozzi, The Conditional Probability Machine. University of St. Andrews, St. Katharines Gallery, February*

1973 Eduardo Paolozzi: Bunk. London, Victoria and Albert Museum (Travelling)

1974 Eduardo Paolozzi, Skulpturen, Reliefs, Zeichnungen, Grafik. Hamburg, Galerie Wentzel, 12 September-28 October

Eduardo Paolozzi, Hannover, Kestner-Gesellschaft, 6 December-19 January 1975*

1975 Eduardo Paolozzi, Skulpturen, Zeichnungen, Collagen, Druckgrafik. Berlin, Staatliche Museen Preussischer Kulturbesitz, Nationalgalerie and Kupferstichkabinett, 5 February-6 April*

Eduardo Paolozzi, Handzeichnungen, Collagen, Druckgrafik. Bremen, Kunsthalle, 17 August-28 September*

1976 Eduardo Paolozzi, New Reliefs and Sculpture. London, Marlborough Fine Art, 30 February-6 March*

Eduardo Paolozzi, Recent Work. Edinburgh, Scottish Arts Council, Fruit Market Gallery, 5 June-3 July*

Eduardo Paolozzi. Swift Current, Saskatchewan, Canada, National Exhibition Centre, 10-31 October

Eduardo Paolozzi. Vancouver, Fine Art Gallery, 15 November-15 December

Eduardo Paolozzi, Sculpture, Drawings, Collages and Graphics. An Arts Council Exhibition, Newcastle, Laing Art Gallery, 17 April-16 May; Edinburgh, Scottish Arts Council Gallery, 29 May-27 June; Leigh, Turnpike Gallery, 3-24 July; Wolverhampton, Municipal Art Gallery, 31 July-29 August; Hull, Ferens Art Gallery, 4 September-3 October; Southampton, Art Gallery, 0. October-14 November*

1977 Eduardo Paolozzi, Sculpture, Drawings, Collages and Graphic. An Arts Council Exhibition, Cardiff, Chapter

Arts Centre, 4-22 January; Kendal, Abbot Hall Gallery, 29 January-26 February*

Eduardo Paolozzi. St. Catherine, Ontario, Rodman Art Centre, 7-31 January

Eduardo Paolozzi. Montreal, Concordia University George Williams Art Gallery, 15 February-15 March

Eduardo Paolozzi, Collages and Drawings. London Anthony d'Offay, 23 March-22 April*

Eduardo Paolozzi. Kingston, Queens University, Etherington Art Gallery, 2-24 April

Eduardo Paolozzi. Frederictown, N.B., Beaverbrook Art Gallery, 14 May-15 June

The Complete Prints of Eduardo Paolozzi – Prints, Drawings, Collages 1944-77. London, Victoria and Albert Museum*

1978 Eduardo Paolozzi, Kleinplastiken, Zeichnungen, Grafik. Kassel, Kasseler Kunstverein, 2 March-7 April*

1979 Eduardo Paolozzi, 'The Development of the Idea'. St. Andrews, University of St. Andrews, Balcony Gallery, 11 May-9 June*

Eduardo Paolozzi, Collages, Prints, Sculptures. Edinburgh, Talbot Rice Art Centre, Edinburgh University, August-22 September*

Eduardo Paolozzi, Work in Progress. Cologne, Kölnischer Kunstverein, 19 Oktober-11 November

1980 Eduardo Paolozzi. Vienna, Galerie 17, 6-19 November

Paolozzi Prints. Münster, Westfälischer Kunstverein

1981 Eduardo Paolozzi, Grafik, Zeichnung, Kleinplastik. Salzburg, Hypobank, 24 July-19 August

1982 Eduardo Paolozzi, Druckgrafik. Hamburg, Deutsche BP, Clubheim, 25 March-23 April

Eduardo Paolozzi und sein Drucker Hans Kästel. Hamburg, Museum für Kunst und Gewerbe, 19 May-July

1983 Eduardo Paolozzi, Kunst und Bau – Architekten Projects. Berlin, Aedes Galerie für Architektur und Raum, 22 February-19 March*

Druckgrafik 1974 bis 1982, Wissenschaftskolleg Berlin, 1 November-19 February

1984 Eduardo Paolozzi, Private Vision. Public Art. London, Architectural Association, 20 February-31 March*

Eduardo Paolozzi, Graphics and Sculpture, Metropole Art Centre, Folkestone, 14 June-September

Eduardo Paolozzi. Edinburgh, The Royal Scottish Academy, 12 August-23 September

Eduardo Paolozzi. Munich, Städtische Galerie Lenbachhaus, 17 October-25 November

1985 Eduardo Paolozzi. Cologne, Museum Ludwig February-24 March

Les Mains éblouies. Paris, Galerie Maeght

Réalités nouvelles. Paris, Palais des Beaux-Arts, 22 July-30 August

Kenneth King / Eduardo Paolozzi / William Turnbull. London, Hanover Gallery, 21 February-18 March

Growth and Form. London, Institute of Contemporary Arts, 4 July-31 August

Adams / Blow / Paolozzi / Pasmore. Rome, Galleria Origine, 8-31 March

26 Biennale, Venice

International Sculpture Competition: The Unknown Political Prisoner. London, The Burlington Galleries, 15-30 January; The Tate Gallery, 14 March-30 April

British Painting and Sculpture. London, Whitechapel Art Gallery, September/October

Collages and Objects. London, Institute of Contemporary Arts, 13 October-20 November

This is Tomorrow. London, Whitechapel Art Gallery, 9 August-9 September

7 Sculptors: Sculpture and Drawings. New York, The Solomon R. Guggenheim Museum, 12 February-20 April

Class of 59. Painting, Sculpture, Collage – Magda Cordell / Eduardo Paolozzi / John McHale. Cambridge, The Union, Cambridge University, 1-19 February

New Images of Man. New York, Museum of Modern Art

Documenta II. Kassel

Beeldententoonstelling Floridae. Rotterdam, Museum Boymans-van Beuningen, 25 March-25 September

39 Biennale. Venice

Davie / Paolozzi / Vaughan. Sao Paulo, VII Bienal de Sao Paulo, September-December

Documenta III. Kassel

Verzameling Sir Edward and Lady Hulton, London. Rotterdam, Museum Boymans-van Beuningen. 27 November-17 January 1965

British Sculpture in the Sixties. London, The Tate Gallery, 25 February-1 April

1966 Englische Graphik. Cologne, Galerie der Spiegel. 20 May-20 June

Sculpture in the Open Air. London, Battersea Park, 20 May-30 September

Blake / Boshier / Caulfield / Hamilton / Paolozzi. Milan, Studio Marconi, June

Jim Dine, Drawings, Collage, Collaborations with Eduardo Paolozzi, Photographic Dreams with Michael Cooper and a 'Tool Box' Screenprinted by Kelpra Studio, 1966. London, Robert Fraser Gallery, 13 September-15 October

International Sculpture Exhibition. New York, The Solomon R. Guggenheim Museum, 20 October-4 February 1968

1968 Ars multiplicata, Vervielfältigungskunst seit 1945. Cologne, Wallraf-Richartz-Museum, 13 January-15 April

L'Art vivant: 1965-1968. Saint Paul de Vence, Fondation Maeght, 13 April-30 June

Documenta IV. Kassel

1969 Pop Art Redefined. London, Hayward Gallery, 9 July-3 September

Neue illustrierte Bücher und Graphikmappen. Frankfurt/M., Frankfurter Kunstverein, 8 October-6 November

75th Exhibition of Painting, Sculpture, Drawing, Applied Art and Architecture. Edinburgh, The Royal Scottish Academy Galleries, 9 October-9 November

1970 International Sculptors, Symposium for Expo '70, Osaka, September-November

3 ∞ : new multiple art. London, Whitechapel Art Gallery, 19 November-3 January 1971

1971 Metamorphose des Dinges, Kunst und Antikunst 1910-1970. Brussels, Palais des Beaux Arts, 22 April-6 June; Rotterdam, Museum Boymans-van Beuningen, 25 June-15 August; Berlin, Nationalgalerie, 15 September-7 November; Milan, Palazzo Reale, 15 December-10 February 1972

Graphik der Welt. Internationale Druckgrapik der letzten 25 Jahre. Nürnberg, Kunsthalle, 28 August-28 November

1972 Metamorphose des Dinges, Kunst und Antikunst 1910-1970. Basel, Kunsthalle, 4 March-22 April; Paris, Musée des Arts Décoratifs, May-June

Weltkulturen und moderne Kunst. Begegnungen der europäischen Kunst mit Asien, Afrika, Ozeanien, Afro- und Indoamerika. Munich, Haus der Kunst, 16 June-30 September

'British Sculptors', Royal Academy of Arts, London

1973 Amerikanische und Englische Graphik der Gegenwart aus der Graphischen Sammlung der Staatsgalerie Stuttgart. Stuttgart, Graphische Sammlung der Staatsgalerie Stuttgart, 17 February-13 March

Graphische Techniken. Berlin, Neuer Berliner Kunstverein, 24 February-24 March

1975 Druckgrafik der Gegenwart 1960-1975. Berlin, Staatliche Museen Preussischer Kulturbesitz, Kupferstichkabinett, 20 June-24 August

1976 Pop Art in England, Anfänge einer neuen Figuration /

Beginning of a New Figuration 1947-63. Hamburg, Kunstverein, 7 February-21 March, Munich Städtische Galerie im Lenbachhaus, 3 April-16 May; York, City Art Gallery, 29 May-11 July

'Arte Inglese Oggi', Palazzo Reale, Milano

11 Internationale Künstler. Gäste des Berliner Künstlerprogramms, Deutscher Akademischer Austauschdienst, im Wissenschaftszentrum Bonn-Bad Godesberg, 12 November-15 December

1977 Documenta 6. Kassel

Hayward Annual, Hayward Gallery, London

Jubilee Sculpture Exhibition, Battersea Park, London

'Kunst – Was ist das?'. Hamburg, Kunsthalle

1978 Europäisches Patentamt Munich, Bildhauerwettbewerb. Munich, Deutsches Museum, 25 December-14 January 1979

'Painters in Parallel', Scottish Arts Association, Edinburgh

1979 Summer Exhibition. London, Royal Academy of Arts, 19 May-12 August

Silver Jubilee Exhibition of Paintings. London, Dulwich Picture Gallery, 17 November-9 December

1980 Mein Kölner Dom, zeitgenössische Künstler sehen den Kölner Dom. Cologne, Kölnischer Kunstverein, 16 October-23 November

'20th Century British Sculpture', Whitechapel Gallery, London

'Sculpture for the Blind', Tate Gallery, London

'Westkunst', Rheinhallen, Cologne

1982 The Print Collection, A Selection. London, The Tate Gallery, March-June

'Out of this World', science fiction exhibition at Brighton Museum

1983 6th International Drawing Biennale, Invited Artist: Eduardo Paolozzi. Cleveland (UK), County Museum

'English Painters 1900-1982', Meueo Municipal of Madrid

'Drawing in Air', Sunderland Art Centre

1984 'The Automobile and Culture' Museum of Contemporary Art, Los Angeles

'Artistic Collaboration in the 20th Century', Hirshhorn Museum, Washington

EXHIBITIONS AND LITERATURE REFERRED TO IN THE CATALOGUE

EXHIBITIONS by location and date

A.C.G.B. 1976-7: Arts Council of Great Britain (touring exhibition) 'Eduardo Paolozzi, sculpture, drawings, collages and graphics'
Berlin 1965: Akademie de Künste, 'Neue Realisten & Pop Art'
Berlin 1969: Galerie Mikro 'Eduardo Paolozzi, complete graphics'
Berlin 1975: Nationalgalerie, 'Eduardo Paolozzi'
Berlin 1983-4: Deutschen Akademischen Ausauschdienstes 'Eduardo Paolozzi, Druckgrafik'
Cologne 1979: Kolnischer Kunstverein 'Eduardo Paolozzi, Work in Progress'
Cologne 1980: Kolnischer Kunstverein, 'Mein Kolner Dom'
Edinburgh 1976: Scottish Arts Council, Fruitmarket Gallery, 'Eduardo Paolozzi, Recent Work'
Edinburgh 1979: Talbot Rice Art Centre, 'Eduardo Paolozzi, Collages, Prints, Sculpture'
Hamburg 1982: Deutschen BP Aktiengesellschaft, 'Eduardo Paolozzi, Drukgrafik'
Hannover 1974-5: Kestner-Gesellschaft, 'Eduardo Paolozzi'
Kassel 1978: Kasseler Kunstverein 'Eduardo Paolozzi, sculpture, drawings and graphics'
London 1947: Mayor Gallery, 'Drawings and Sculptures by Eduardo Paolozzi'
London 1954: Institute of Contemporary Arts, 'Collages and Objects'
London 1958: Hanover Gallery, 'Paolozzi, sculpture'
London 1963: The Waddington Galleries, 'Paolozzi New Works'
London 1967: Hanover Gallery, 'Eduardo Paolozzi, sculpture and graphics'
London 1971: Tate Gallery, 'Eduardo Paolozzi'
London 1973: Victoria and Albert Museum, 'Eduardo Paolozzi, Bunk'
London 1976: Marlborough Fine Art, 'Eduardo Paolozzi, New Reliefs and Sculpture'
London 1977: Victoria and Albert Museum, 'The Complete Prints of Eduardo Paolozzi'

London 1977 (2): Anthony d'Offay, 'Eduardo Paolozzi, Collages and Drawings'
London 1981: Tate Gallery, 'Sculpture for the Blind'
London 1984: The Architectural Association, 'Eduardo Paolozzi, Private Vision – Public Art'
Newcastle 1965: Hatton Gallery, The University of Newcastle-upon-Tyne, 'Eduardo Paolozzi, Recent Sculpture, Drawings and Collages'
New York 1958: Solomon R. Guggenheim Museum, 'Sculptures and Drawings from Seven Sculptors'
New York 1960: Betty Parsons Gallery, 'Paolozzi'
New York 1962: Betty Parsons Gallery, 'Paolozzi'
Oxford 1982: Ashmolean Museum, 'Innovations in Contemporary Printmaking'
St. Andrews 1979: Crawford Centre, University of St. Andrews, 'The Development of the Idea'
Stuttgart 1969: Wurtembergischer Kunsverein, 'Eduardo Paolozzi, Plastiken, graphik'

LITERATURE
Hamilton, R., 'Interview with Eduardo Paolozzi', **Arts Yearbook**, 8, 1965.
Kirkpatrick, D., **Eduardo Paolozzi**, London 1970.
Konnertz, W., **Eduardo Paolozzi**, Cologne 1984.
Middleton, M., **Eduardo Paolozzi**, London 1963.
Paolozzi, E., 'Where Reality Lies', **The Oxford Art Journal**, Vol. 6, no. 1, 1983, pp. 39-44.
Reichardt, J., 'Recent Work by Contemporary Artists', **Metro**, Milan, No. 8, Jan.-Mar. 1963, pp. 78-87.
Reichardt, J., 'Eduardo Paolozzi', **Studio International**, Vol. 168, Oct. 1964, pp. 152-157.
Roditi, E., **Dialogues on Art**, Santa Barbara 1980 (first ed. 1960).
Schneede, U.M., **Paolozzi**, New York 1970.
Sotheby's, Catalogue of sale of Impressionist, Modern and Contemporary Paintings, Sculpture and Drawings, Part II, 24 March 1983.
Whitford, F., 'Paolozzi' – Radio-Vision booklet published by the BBC for their 'Art and Design' series, 1971.

C1.3